Think Fast
Speak Smart

How to think and speak brilliantly in impromptu situations

SOLOMON ASINE

For permission requests, write to the publisher at:

info@homeofinfluence.com

Think Fast Speak Smart is a product of Home of Influence LLC

Manufactured in the United States of America

First Printing, 2020

ISBN: 978-1-7351977-0-8

www.homeofinfluence.com

This book is dedicated to my wife Tamarra, and my brother Chris.

CONTENTS

Introduction

What if a brilliant response to an unexpected question is what changes everything?

In 1997, Apple's co-founder Steve Jobs returned to take on the job as CEO at Apple over a decade after he had left the same company in 1985. Before Jobs left Apple, he, along with some other employees of the company, worked on developing the Macintosh computer. This was after he was kicked out of the project Lisa, a computer he named after his daughter. He started and ran the Macintosh project almost as a separatist group within Apple. He selected and organized a team of hardworking, dedicated, and talented engineers. This was an act of rebellion for being kicked out of the project Lisa. He often referred to this team as "pirates." According to Jobs, "It is better to be a pirate than to be in the navy." The team basically became a separate group within Apple.

Eventually, the Macintosh computer was launched on the 24th of January 1984. Macintosh had great tech reviews and hype, and there were a lot of revs around the product. Unfortunately, the sales fell short of expectation under Jobs, and in 1985 sales began to plummet. This unexpected decline in sales increased the already existing strain between Jobs and John Sculley, the CEO of Apple at the time, who had a different vision for the company. And in May of 1985, Sculley initiated the reorganization of the company with the backing of the directors. The restructuring rid Jobs of his influence at Apple and left him with a non-operational position. Jobs likened his new role to living in Siberia. On September 17, 1985, Steve Jobs submitted his resignation letter to the board.

So, when he returned to Apple in 1997, 12 years after he was kicked off, it wasn't like the return of a savior. Many resented him because of his attitude and the way he left the company.

Also, at that time, Apple was in a deep financial crisis, and not everybody believed that Jobs was the right man to bring the much-needed change. Jobs needed to gain the confidence of everybody.

At the Apple Worldwide Developers Conference, while on stage, Jobs had a Q&A session with developers. During this session, an audience member stood up and not only asked a question but also insulted him.

Audience member:
"It's sad and clear that on several counts you've discussed, you don't know what you're talking about— [Audience laughter]. I would like, for example, for you to express in clear terms how, say, Java and any of its incarnations addresses the ideas embodied in OpenDoc. And when you're finished with that, perhaps you can tell us what you personally have been doing for the last seven years."

The hall fell into complete silence, except for the voice of someone who uttered "Ouch." A sound that I believe is a reaction to the question that anyone could interpret as an insult.

What followed was a masterpiece impromptu speech. Jobs' response was a classic example of how to graciously transform an "insult-based question" to a significant reinforcement of a vision.

Steve Jobs:
"You know, you can please some of the people some of the time, but one of the hardest things when you're trying to effect change is that people like this gentleman are right in some areas. I'm sure that there are somethings OpenDoc does, probably even more that I am not familiar with that nothing out there does. And I am sure that you can make some demos, maybe a small commercial app that demonstrates those things"

"The hardest thing is: how does that fit into a cohesive, larger vision, that's going to allow you to sell 8 billion dollars, 10 billion dollars of product a year? And, one of the things I've always found is that you've got to start with the customer experience and work backwards for the technology. You can't start with the technology and try to figure out where you're going to try to sell it. And I made this mistake probably more than anybody else in this room. And I got the scar tissue to prove it. And I know that it's the case," Jobs said.

"And as we have tried to come up with a strategy and a vision for Apple, it started with 'What incredible benefits can we give to the customer? Where can we take the customer?' Not starting with 'Let's sit down with the engineers and figure out what awesome technology we have and then how are we going to market that?' And I think that's the right path to take…" Jobs continued.

"Mistakes will be made, some people will be pissed off, some people will not know what they're talking about, but I think it's so much better than where things were not very long ago. And I think we're going to get there." Jobs concludes.

What a response! This moment and many others were critical in reviving the confidence and trust stakeholders and employees at Apple had in him.

What About You?
What if you could give such a brilliant response in times when it matters most? Sadly, that is not the case for most people.

Can you think of a time when you struggled to get your point across to an audience, maybe in a group interaction or during a presentation? Such moments are often typical in times when you are not prepared to speak. However, when you think of other times when you were prepared, you can tell that your performance was much better.

The reality is that your thoughts and ideas are often well organized and presented when you have the time to think and prepare for what you want to say or present. For example, when you are preparing for an important networking event, you are likely to take out time to think through the kind of questions you would ask and how to answer specific questions that are common in such environment. In these moments, you choose the very best lines with which you speak. This is not the case when you don't have the opportunity to prepare before speaking. When you are caught unaware, you tend to experience distortion in your thought process, especially when your audience is sizeable. In such moments you are not as constructive with your message as you would hope to be.

There are a lot of people who still struggle to speak with clarity and precision. Many people avoid places where they believe they might have to speak impromptu. They hide behind this flaw. And painfully enough, many people don't even think that they can be good at impromptu speaking. I have interviewed several people who don't even want to discuss the subject. It is disturbing to see. I find it sad because I know how possible it is to move from mediocrity to excellence in the delivery of impromptu speeches. I know how it feels to speak intelligently in unfamiliar and unexpected situations, especially as someone who was once inept at it.

I don't think this is the kind of skill that anybody should ignore, because you strengthen your reputation when you speak well in impromptu situations. This even more important for anyone who is a leader or hopes to occupy a leadership position. You will agree with me that great leaders are excellent communicators. Firmly integrated into their skillset, is the ability to communicate excellently well. They can speak well when they are caught off guard and are unprepared. The ability to think on your feet is an essential skill to have, and most of them possess it. (Mind you, not all leaders are good at impromptu speaking).

The truth is that occasions where you are required to think and speak on your feet, like responding to questions or supporting an opinion, debating, etc., will never cease to present themselves, especially as you move up the rungs of life's ladder. It is not something that you can hide from, no matter what you do or how introverted or shy you are. As you go through life, you inevitably come head-on with situations where you are required to speak on your feet. It is your choice to make a mess of these moments or be outstanding.

Sometimes it may seem like the skill of effective impromptu speaking comes naturally to some people, but that is not the case. Some people grew up in environments where they are allowed to express themselves freely. Some other people grew up in homes where they are to be seen but not heard. There is no doubt that the environment we grow up in plays a role in shaping our expressiveness as adults, but it is not the sole determinant. I have come across many intelligent and smart speakers that are good with impromptu speaking. When I ask most of them how they became competent in the art, the majority said that they had a lot of exposure to situations where they spoke regularly. It took them time and practice to get there.

For almost a decade, I have been studying the art of persuasive communication, and I have had the privilege to review the art of impromptu speaking carefully. I have compiled valuable techniques on how to master the art of impromptu speaking. In this book, I am going to share these techniques with you. My goal is to see that you grow exponentially in your ability to think and speak intelligently on your feet.

So, if you desire to strengthen this vital communication skill, then you must get ready because this book is going to teach you all the tricks you need to know. Studying and practicing the lessons in this book will help you bridge the gap between the quality of your prepared speeches and your impromptu speeches, ultimately enhancing your impromptu speaking skills. So, as you navigate through and glean from the pages of this book, you will find critical precepts that you need to help you handle impromptu speeches logically and intelligently.

CHAPTER ONE

Uncovering the wounds

And finally, Lincoln was not a good impromptu speaker; he was at his best when he could read from a carefully prepared manuscript. Though maybe a teleprompter could have helped that!

-David Herbert Donald

Michael was a 22-year-old with exceptional talents and academic successes. He was a graduate in engineering from the prestigious Duke University. Just after he graduated, Michael was employed to work at Devon Inc., a company he had always wished to work for. So, being an employee at Devon was a dream come true. He was enjoying his life, and there was nothing better he could ask for. He loved his new job; it was a unique experience for him, and he savored every moment of it.

Following a formal procedure, Jimmy Perry, the CEO of Devon, called to meet with the new employees. At his request, the new members of staff were seated in a meeting room, and among them was Michael. The CEO hoped to find out more about those who were going to be a part of the company's future.

Just as any passionate chief executive would do, Jimmy spent the first ten minutes talking about Devon, its past, present, and future. Sitting to his far-right was Michael. He sat there quietly, digesting every single word that left his boss's mouth. He felt like he was a part of something great. But this feeling was distorted, as least temporarily, when he heard his name. Jimmy called on him and asked him a question, "Michael, how do you see the future of engineering, and how relevant do you think you would be in shaping that future?" For a moment, Michael's thoughts were scattered all around, like the crumbs from a cake littered on the floor. His memory became as blank as a freshly opened Word document. At that moment, he would have preferred to have a rock tied to his back and dumped in the middle of the ocean than to endure the bitterness of his current situation. He knew so much about engineering and obviously how to answer the question. But unfortunately, when put on the spot, he could think of so little. His heart was racing faster than his thoughts. It was probably through sheer luck that he responded to the question; however, his response was rash and uncoordinated. He answered without much confidence.

Michael loved his job, but not on this day. He spent the entire day beating himself up, thinking of how unorganized the content of his response was, thinking of what Jimmy and his colleagues made of him. He thought of possible reasons why he could not answer a question that was supposed to be an easy one on a typical day. If only he could turn back the hands of time, he would right this wrong.

****

Joseph was a decent man with a loving wife and two beautiful children. At 35, he had many stories to tell about friends. Stories of how they can betray you and stories of how loyal, reliable, trustworthy, and supportive, good friends can be. Marx was of the latter. He was Joseph's best friend. A loyal, trustworthy, and reliable friend. They had been through a lot together, both in good times and in bad times.

Both friends had a lot in common, but one difference was that Marx was single. He was so devoted to his career that he thought getting married would be a distraction. This mind-set was altered when he found the love of his life. Now, all he could think about was spending the rest of his life with her. And so, at 34, Marx finally decided to get married.

It was a day that many people prayed to witness, especially Joseph. At Marx's wedding reception, Joseph, as a groomsman, was extremely excited. He was eating, drinking, and having a good time. While the ceremony advanced, he was having conversations with friends and well-wishers.

Joseph was in a deep conversation with a well-wisher when he heard his name, not from his conversation partner, but from the master of ceremony. In that moment, the sound of his name was distressing to his ears. It came like an arrow and completely deflated his conversation. "Please, let's welcome Joseph, a good friend of the groom." Joseph's mood quickly changed from sweet to sour. "Could you please come and tell this beautiful audience something about your friend?" the master of ceremony continued. This was more dreadful than his scariest nightmare. Joseph was never a good public speaker, so this was a bad moment for him. He was completely overshadowed with fear. It took him some time to stand up from his seat. And as he walked towards the microphone, he felt nauseated, near the point of throwing up. The microphone was heavy—heavier than normal—and when he looked at the audience, he was the center of attention. It felt like a thousand unfriendly eyes were looking sternly into his soul, patiently waiting for him to make a fool of himself.

At this point, Joseph could barely control his thoughts. But the fact was that he knew more about Marx than any other person in that audience. He had a lot to say about Marx, but in that moment, it felt like the part of his brain holding that information had been eaten up by maggots. It was only after about 30 seconds (which seemed like hours) that he was able to speak. He murmured several uncoordinated words, words that fell very short of how much he knew about his good friend. And the rest was history; he was a disappointment. The rest of that day was soured by this brief moment of shame. He spent the entire day thinking of all the good things he knew about Marx and what he should have said. It was just as if the maggots had regurgitated his brains.

Beyond Stories

These are not just stories. There are a lot of people who will tell you how difficult it is for them to speak impromptu. You may think words are cheap and easily accessible, but the right words could be very scarce in times when they are urgently needed. You can liken such moments to searching for water in the middle of a desert; it is always a heart-wrenching experience.

The frustration is shared not just by Michael and Joseph, but by many people around the world. People who avoid discussion groups and other forms of gathering because they fear to speak. People who missed great opportunities simply because they couldn't speak up or give an effective response to a question. People who desire to be competent at speaking effectively in an impromptu situation.

Let me share with you a few of the many reactions that I have received about impromptu speaking.

"I hate being called upon to address people when I am not ready. I always mess things up" –Grace

"If you want to make me sick, just call me to speak when I am not prepared."-Victoria

"There is no other time that my heart beats the most."- Samuel

"Sometimes, I feel like I can never be good at speaking impromptu."-John

"I shrink when I hear impromptu. I was once embarrassed on national TV for my poor response to a question."-Efosa

The cases are endless.

You may share the same burden with those mentioned above, or you may have put in the work to get better with speaking, but the most important thing is that you should not allow the fact that you struggle with impromptu speaking plague your life.

The pages of this book are filled with instructions and useful guidelines that would drag you out of the rut of mediocrity into the realm of excellence when it comes down to a smooth delivery of impromptu speeches. The ability to speak off-the-cuff, logically and intelligently, is one essential skill that you should strive to possess. Merikare, an ancient Egyptian pharaoh of the 10th Dynasty, was quoted for saying, "Be skillful in speech, that you may be strong." I agree with this quote. No matter who you are or what you do, you will always be at an advantage and in a better position if you possess this remarkable skill.

But before I go further, it is important to go a bit deeper into what an impromptu speech is. Why is the art of speaking impromptu an essential skill in the field of communication? Why is it essential to develop this skill? What are the possible scenarios that could put you on the spot to deliver an impromptu speech? It is crucial to have answers to these questions to appreciate the process that this book will take you through.

What Is an Impromptu Speech?
The Oxford Advanced Leaner's dictionary defines the term impromptu as anything done without preparation or planning. Going by this definition, an impromptu speech is a speech that is delivered off-the-cuff, meaning, without enough time to prepare. In this definition, the use of the phrase "enough time to prepare" simply suggests that there is time to prepare for an impromptu speech. But in this case, it is not your usual preparation, and the time is limited.

The time for preparation here is the few seconds to minutes that you need to assemble your thoughts and ideas most logically. The time required for preparation can be as short as an average of 5 seconds in the case of an interview, or longer, in cases where you have to walk down to a podium. You may even have a longer time to prepare; for example, a ceremony or event host might ask you to stand-in for someone who was scheduled to speak but is unavailable. This situation is also called extemporaneous speaking. In any case, for an impromptu speech, you are expected to deliver your thought to an audience in a logical and organized manner without prior notice.

We Do This Everyday

It is almost impossible for one to go through a day without giving a speech in one form or another, whether you are aware of it or not. It can be as simple as describing your experience at a zoo or saying something about a movie you saw or describing how you spent your day or weekend. It can also be as elaborate and technical as speaking for about five minutes or more about inflation in your country or why you think your company can outperform a more significant competition. What you must understand is that your daily conversations are filled with impromptu speeches. It is particularly true in corporate settings, where team members brainstorm on ideas, multiple discussions take place within focus groups, meeting after meeting are scheduled, and there is generally a high level of verbal communication.

Note that with general reference to speeches, what differentiates an impromptu speech from other types of speeches is its length, its unexpectedness, the fact that it is a short speech, and because you don't always deliver it in a formal or organized setting. You are going to see as you read further that an impromptu speech embodies the most basic unit of a regular speech structure. Also, an impromptu speech can be informative. It can serve a persuasive purpose. It can be delivered to entertain and even to motivate.

Impromptu Speaking Situations

As I have mentioned, along the course of your daily life, you will face several situations that would require you to speak off-the-cuff. These situations are unavoidable, especially if you interact with humanity and if you desire to make meaning out of your life. Unfortunately, or maybe I should say, fortunately, as your corporate and other responsibilities increase, you will inevitably fall into diverse situations that would require you to speak impromptu. The option for you is either to ace the speeches as they present themselves or to flop. It is not anybody's desire to face a series of embarrassment from impromptu speaking gaffes. So, your best bet is to ace them. Impromptu speaking situations are numerous. Below are some common scenarios.

- You may find yourself in a panel answering questions from an audience.
- You may be called upon to give a toast that you did not prepare for.
- You may have to answer questions in an interview, maybe for a job, on television, radio, telephone, etc.
- You may have to respond to questions in a Q&A session after your presentation.
- You may need to answer unexpected and difficult questions in a one-on-one conversation, maybe on a first date, a networking event, etc.
- An event host might ask you to stand-in for an unavailable speaker.
- You may be called upon to say a few words after a meeting, or any other special gathering.
- After pitching your idea, you might get a question that you did not anticipate.
- Someone might ask you your point of view on an issue in a meeting or other public setting.

The situations are numerous, and your audience can range from one person to a large crowd of people.

Benefits of Impromptu Speaking Skills

I don't think there is anybody that wouldn't want to improve their ability to speak without a glitch when placed in the spotlight. Especially knowing how embarrassing it could be when someone asks you to say a few words or to share your view in a meeting or to give an impromptu toast, and you make a mess of the situation. There is hardly anyone who has not at one time or the other been in this position. The truth is that your reputation is strengthened anytime you speak in a clear and well-organized manner, and conversely, you put a dent on your reputation when you mess things up. When you become competent in this art, several benefits follow.

- It could be what land you the next job opportunity or sale, etc.
- You are more likely to get a promotion than your colleagues.
- You can verbally express your thoughts logically and coherently.
- You will enhance your ability to think quickly on your feet.
- People want to be around you and listen to you.
- You will develop a high level of confidence in public speaking.
- You will strengthen your competence in communication.
- You will improve your verbal fluency.
- You won't be afraid or shy to expose yourself to settings where someone might ask you to speak.
- You will increase your confidence level and ultimately improve your outlook on life.

These benefits must not be overlooked by anyone who knows how important it is to communicate effectively, especially those who are pursuing a career or those who are in leadership positions. Take note also that to enjoy these benefits, you must be ready to increasingly expose yourself to places where you are likely to speak impromptu. You should approach your growth as a speaker with a conscious effort, that way, you can track your progress and ultimately appreciate the process.

Why Is This Chapter Important?

I wrote this chapter not only to make you see impromptu speaking for what it is but also to shed light on the facts, to unravel the pain, to make you understand that you are not alone in the struggle.

Michael, the young man in the opening story, was brilliant. You will be right to call him an exceptional engineer, but his ineptitude in the area of impromptu speaking was a weakness, and it affected his credibility. It gave his emotions a hard knock, and he also experienced a bitter day, one that he may never forget.

Also, Joseph, the character mentioned in my second story, was a victim of this weakness, a weakness that caused him to experience temporal mental disorientation. His age did not save him. His love for his friend Marx did not help him on that podium. His knowledge of his dear friend disappeared from his memory when it was needed the most. It is a sad experience!

The fact is that Michael, Joseph, and the other names mentioned are not alone in this struggle. There is a vast global community of individuals that still share in this pain. Some are young, and some are old, some are professionals, and some are laymen. There is a chance that you also struggle to articulate your thoughts intelligently. But there is good news! You can drastically improve the nimbleness of your mind and the precision of your thoughts. You can have a sigh of relief. Just take note of all the secrets that I am about to share with you, put them together, and digest them. When you do, you will find yourself rising above the crowd. All you need to do is sit back, relax, and READ ON!

CHAPTER TWO

Facing Your Fears

What is needed, rather than running away or controlling or suppressing or any other resistance, is understanding fear; that means, watch it, learn about it, come directly into contact with it. We are to learn about fear, not how to escape from it.

-Jiddu Krishnamurti

"Within seconds of perceiving a threat, the primitive amygdala sounds a general alarm. The adrenal system promptly floods the body with adrenaline and stress hormones. Nonessential physiological processes switch off. Digestion stops, skin chills, and blood is diverted into muscles in preparation for a burst of emergence action. Breathing quickens, the heart races, and blood pressure skyrockets, infusing the body with oxygen while the liver releases glucose for quick fuel. The entire body is suddenly in a state of high alert, ready for fight or flight."

The description above sounds terrifying, but that is the truth about fear. That is what it does to you. It paralyzes you. It destabilizes you; it makes you lose your reasoning, and it makes you act irrationally. Fear is a tormentor.

Why do I address the subject of fear in this book? Why is it essential to talk about fear when it comes to the question of effectiveness in delivering impromptu speeches? Simple! Fear is often the foundation of failure in any form of public speaking. It is the origin of the mental disorientation that a lot of people experience when they find themselves unexpectedly in the spotlight. Painfully, many people are victims of the fear of public speaking.

There is a popular saying that *the fear of public speaking is greater than the fear of death.* I can't tell you how accurate this statement is; however, I can imagine that. Fear can cripple the mind, temporarily distorting or erasing its contents, and leaving its victim helpless. Therefore, taking a closer look at fear or anxiety, and ways of dealing with it, is of critical importance in the subject of impromptu speaking.

When you manage your fears successfully, your mind becomes clear enough to handle the quick and logical flow that is required to deliver a sound and effective impromptu speech.

I Was a Victim

I think fear is a fascinating subject. I find it interesting not only because of how damaging it is to its victim but because of the experience that initiated my transition from a fearful public speaker to a confident one.

I still remember the day when I had a close encounter with public speaking anxiety. It was a day that made me think deeply about fear, especially as it relates to public speaking.

It was my second year in college. It was supposed to be a typical day in class, where my routine was to pay close attention to the subject matter and take down relevant notes. But this day was different.

A lecturer walked into the classroom; he didn't say much before writing on the chalkboard. He wrote just two words: "Chemical Reactions." That was the subject of the day.

He started teaching on the subject, explaining as much as he could about chemical reactions. I was all ears. He went on for about five minutes, then I heard the word "You," pointing his finger in my direction. I looked behind me, not too sure who he was pointing at. "Why are you looking around?" he said. "I mean you." This time, it was clear. I was in the spotlight. "In continuation of our subject on chemical reactions, stand up and tell us what you understand by the rate of a chemical reaction?" That was it. All hell broke loose, both in my head and all over my body. The fact that everyone's attention was on me, waiting for me to answer the question, made me so anxious to the extent that my body began to react in strange ways. I felt my eyes turn red, and a sudden weakness on my knees. I could feel my stomach muscles cramping. My throat became parched, and my heart was racing at record speed. I honestly can't think of any other similar experience. I stood there like a dead log. I remember saying some words, but it would have been better if all I did was shut up, because everything I said was gibberish.

When I finally sat down, I was exhausted. I felt like that short moment drained more energy from me than mowing a ten-thousand-square-foot lawn would have. It was a terrible experience.

My answer to the question was dumb, not because I did not know the answer, but only because I allowed fear to overshadow my thought. It was a very humiliating moment for me, one that I would never forget.

There Is Hope

If you always find yourself fearful when asked to speak, fear not, for you are not alone. There are people who would rather jump down from a cliff than stand before an audience to speak. That would have been a better option for me at that moment. This illustration may sound exaggerated, but you will be surprised to find out how true that is.

Going back, one would ask the question, why was I so fearful? There was no visible force that triggered the dramatic body reaction I experienced; it was just a matter of my state of mind. According to Napoleon Hill, "Fears are nothing more than a state of mind." In the latter part of the chapter, I will share with you one of the ways I overcame my fear of public speaking, which had to do with readjusting my state of mind. When I overcame this fear, I discovered how ridiculous it is to get uncontrollably anxious when asked to speak.

The good news is that anyone can learn to manage their fear of public speaking. I used the word "manage" because you can still speak very effectively even when you are nervous. According to Georges St-Pierre, a former Welterweight Champion, "It's okay to get butterflies in your stomach; the key is to learn how to make them fly in formation." I would support this quote with another quote by Mark Twain "There are two types of speakers, those that are nervous and those that are liars." Your effort should be directed more towards understanding and managing fear rather than eliminating it, at least for a start.

Fear is just a mirage. It is not real. It is okay to get scared when someone asks you to confront a lunatic that is holding a gun or when you walk into a lion's den without any form of protection. This is because you could get shot by a real bullet as you've probably seen in real life or a movie, or you could get eaten up by a real lion because you understand that they are carnivores. But being scared because someone asked you to say some words is ridiculous. Think about this for a moment.

To have a brighter and more in-depth insight into the subject of fear, we must address it. In the following sections, we are going to stroll around the dark corners of the fear of public speaking, illuminating it with our knowledge of its impotence and its true nature. To begin, you must look within yourself.

Find Out What Scares You

The truth is that most of the time, our fears have no root; they start and stop with our imagination. The best thing to do is to figure out what scares you. Some people would say, "When I speak, everybody judges and accesses me" or "I hate it when all eyes are on me." Some people see it as too isolating when they stand alone or when they are the only ones involved in an activity; in this case, speaking. Such people thrive in communal activities, where they are just a part of the crowd. Other people hate being judged or scrutinized. Some others believe that they are not competent or good enough.

The important thing here is to identify the things that make you scared to speak when the light is on you. You can find out the reason why you get anxious by asking the following questions:

- How does the environment affect your feelings? The

novelty of the speaking situation may cause anxiety. If it's an environment where you are speaking for the first time, the unfamiliarity of the audience or the setting may throw you off balance. If this is what scares you, it is not uncommon. The truth is that there is always some level of anxiety when the members of the audience are unfamiliar or when the size of the audience is much larger than what you are used to. So, you don't have to worry.

- Are you always consumed with what the outcome of your speech would be? It could be that you have a fear of failure; you so desire success that the thought of not speaking well causes you to fear. It could also be that you just feel incompetent and believe that you will sound inarticulate or bore the audience. Or maybe you are just scared of the feeling of shame and disgrace that comes with poor delivery. Just know that it is only through failure that you can achieve true success. So, fear not.

- How does the size of the audience affect the magnitude of your fear? For example, you may be very confident when asked to speak in the presence of just two people or maybe an audience of ten. However, when the audience grows into hundreds of people, you get consumed with fear. The same words that will motivate ten people can also motivate a thousand people. And note, the human eyes are not arrows; they won't strike you when they multiply. Fear not.

- How would you describe your fear as it relates to the quality of the audience? By quality, I mean, how specialized your audience members are. Is it an audience of highly qualified professionals, or is it an audience of non-professionals? The reason for your fear could be that the audience members are more knowledgeable than you. This shouldn't be a reason to fear. Your response, no matter the situation, is based on what you know, and what you understand about the subject matter. You should be confident about this. And if there is a contrary opinion to what you know, then whoever holds that opinion should express their concern for your benefit and the benefit of everyone listening. So, fear not.

- Your fear could just be a fundamental case of a lack of confidence and low self-esteem. If this is the case, then you must make building up your self-confidence your first line of action. When you have a healthy self-esteem, it drastically reduces your anxiety during social interactions and in other public speaking settings. And when your anxiety reduces, your ability to reason logically increases.

There could be other reasons (reasons not highlighted above) why you get scared when you find yourself in an impromptu situation. The first thing you need to do is identify whatever brings out that fear. When you do this, it becomes easier for you to deal with the situation.

Managing Your Fear

Like I mentioned earlier, what you want to do is manage your fears. Some professional speakers still feel some level of anxiety, especially when they are asked to speak without notice. So, as I have said, your effort should be to understand and manage the situation. Consider the following tips to help you manage the fear of speaking.

Speak More Often

I know you think this is ridiculous! In your mind, you are thinking "How do you expect me to speak more often when I am scared to speak?" But the truth is, a significant step in managing your fears is to face them head-on. When you avoid what you fear, it continues to torment you. However, when you face it, you realize it's not as harmful as you believed. This is true with public speaking as it is with any other kind of fear.

Let's call this "exposure." According to W. Clement Stone,

"Thinking will not overcome fear, but action will." Exposure involves gradually and repeatedly going into feared situations until you feel less anxious. Exposure is not dangerous and will not make the fear worse. When you regularly expose yourself to such an environment, your anxiety will naturally lessen. Exposing yourself to various impromptu speaking situations will drastically increase your confidence level. This is a very practical and powerful way to manage fear. Face it head-on.

While trying this approach, you might face challenges, especially at the beginning. Don't get discouraged. Before long, you will become a "fearless" speaker. Always take advantage of any opportunity to speak. Make valid contributions in meetings and other kinds of group settings, call in on live broadcasts to contribute, offer to join discussion panels, etc. When you talk more often, it becomes easy for you to respond coherently without fear when you have to speak impromptu.

Another recommendation is to join Toastmasters international club. Toastmasters is an organization that helps individuals improve their public speaking and leadership skills through practice and feedback. They have what is called Table Topic sessions. In these sessions, they ask you random questions, and you are required to respond in one to two minutes. This is an excellent platform to help you manage your fear.

In summary, make this your mantra: "The more I speak, the less I fear."

Breathe
Breathe! Did you say "breathe"? Yes, breathe. I understand that highlighting the subject of breathing as a recipe for managing fear might sound unconventional to you, but it is imperative. When fear strikes before or during public speaking, your stomach muscles constrict, causing you to breathe from your chest region. This kind of breathing is called thoracic breathing or shallow breathing. When you breathe this way, you draw a small amount of air into your chest region using the intercostal muscles. When this happens, your lungs are starved

of the amount of oxygen that it requires for top performance.

To breathe correctly, you have to fill up your lungs with air by contracting your diaphragm. This kind of breathing is called diaphragmatic breathing or deep breathing. Deep breathing is recommended because it helps to reduce public speaking anxiety. When you breathe from the diaphragm, you send enough oxygen to your lungs, which is then distributed evenly across the body. This increases the amount of oxygen that the brain receives and ultimately improves its performance. Apart from the sufficient oxygen distribution, deep breathing also increases the strength and quality of your voice. It results in powerful projection and resonance.

If you find yourself in an impromptu situation that gives you a little time to prepare, like the case where you need to stand-in for an unavailable speaker, and you get struck by fear, you could use several breathing and relaxation techniques to stay calm. For example, you can stand straight, inhale deeply, and stretch your arms and legs. Then exhale as you bend to touch your toes. Repeat this several times. When you do this exercise, it would ease the tension in your body and hence reduce your anxiety.

Prepare Well

Yes, you read that correctly. Prepare Well. The idea of preparing or practicing for an impromptu speech might seem out of place, but it is not. There are a lot of ways that you can practice impromptu speaking. I dedicated a chapter to practicing for impromptu speeches. One reason people become fearful when faced with speaking before an audience is a lack of preparation. The more knowledge you have on how to deliver an impromptu speech, and the more you practice, the more confident you will be before your audience. You must take out time to practice and prepare yourself. I will discuss that in a later chapter.

Change Your Thoughts About Impromptu Speaking

The way you see impromptu speaking will determine how you

react to it. You must understand that confidence in any form of public speaking is not the exclusive preserve of a select few. You must let go of the mindset that only certain people are naturally gifted with the confidence to speak in public, and that you aren't one of them. This is far from the truth. The ability to speak with confidence is available to anyone willing and diligent enough to understand and practice the rudiments of the art. When you believe you can excel at impromptu speaking and overcome your fears, the process becomes easier. When you start thinking this way, it becomes easier to understand and overcome this irrational fear. This is where I began to conquer my fear of public speaking. I simply had a change of mindset, and my confidence began to increase.

Speak Naturally
When you speak with your natural voice and style, you think less of how your voice sounds or how you would maintain an accent that is not naturally yours. Your thought would be on what you have to say and how to present your points. Keeping your natural voice reduces anxiety and helps you speak better and in a more organized manner. But you must take note that it is okay to work on your voice. You can work on your natural speaking voice to make it powerful, more colorful, and more vibrant. But attempting to speak with an unfamiliar accent in an impromptu speech situation could distract you.

This might not apply to everyone, but it is true for those uncomfortable speaking in their natural voices. This discomfort with the natural voice can also significantly undermine confidence. Therefore, it's essential to accept your natural speaking voice as it is. However, you can work on it to make it crisp, clear, and vibrant.

Skills Training
Attending training on public speaking is an excellent way to develop a better understanding of the art and to overcome the anxiety that comes with it. Again, I strongly recommend joining a Toastmasters club.

That you are reading this book is also a form of skills training. But more important than just reading is the implementation of the precept contained within this book.

Don't Give Fear a Chance

It was Jocelyn Selim that described the anatomy of fear in the opening paragraph of this chapter, which is an excerpt from a 2003 issue of Discover Magazine. It reveals to us what fear does, not just to your mind but also your body. Just imagine; your body flooded with stress hormones, a halt in your digestion process, your skin chilling, your breath rising, your heart racing, your blood pressure rising, and your body in a state of high, red alert. This is not to mention other negative effects on your body, especially your hands, shaking uncontrollably, the dizziness, the light-headedness, a weakened joint, to mention a few. All because you want to say a few words in front of other humans like yourself. You are better than that. Don't give fear such enormous power and control over your body and mind. You are stronger than fear. Do not give fear a chance.

CHAPTER THREE

Understanding the Rubric

Good order is the foundation of all great things
-David Herbert Donald

I was once invited by the Founder and CEO of a small business to attend the company's luncheon, during which I was scheduled to give a brief remark. It was an occasion to celebrate their end of year business achievements. According to him, this was not the first end of year celebration, but I'm yet to attend an event so chaotic, disorganized and unplanned like I did that night. Everything was upside down; I mean everything. The moderator wasn't sure which activity came after which, even though he was holding a white sheet of paper that I assumed was the agenda for the event. Throughout the entire event, they kept apologizing to the audience for mistakes and oversights. I thought to myself, even if this is the first event they've ever had, it shouldn't be this disorganized.

The Need for Structure

Think of the chaotic scenario described above as having a meeting without an agenda. Think about that. When you attempt to hold a meeting without an agenda, there is most likely going to be a lack of coordination, and it would be difficult to tell how such a meeting will eventually turn out. On the contrary, when there is an agenda and a plan, and when that plan is followed, there is an assurance that the meeting will not only proceed smoothly but eventually come to a successful end. This is true not only for meetings and events but also for impromptu speeches. When your response to a question, or any other form of impromptu speaking is without order, it loses its logical flow, and ultimately, your message becomes difficult for the listener or audience to follow and grasp.

Have you ever seen or been around someone who always speaks logically, in a well-organized and intelligent manner? Sometimes it makes you hold the person in high esteem because you admire their level of intelligence. The truth is that we love those who are persuasive with words, those individuals that are coherent and well-spoken.

When you take a closer look at these persuasive talks, what you will see are simple structures. Lengthier speeches also embody these structures. The structure is what creates the logical flow that you feel and enjoy in a speech. An impromptu speech is, therefore, nothing more than a mini speech. Meaning, it has a structure consisting of an opening or introduction, a body, and a conclusion. It embodies a basic model that can be used in a wide variety of speeches.

When you understand this, it provides a clear direction as you sift through ideas to quickly organize your thoughts for an impromptu speech in the limited seconds or minutes available. When you have this in mind, you can stay on track when speaking, and it becomes difficult to derail or ramble off-topic.

If you are still intrigued by the fact that impromptu speeches have the same structure as regular speeches, don't worry; there are examples to help understand and appreciate the flow. But first, let us look at the parts of the structure to understand the role they play.

The Introduction/Opening

The introduction of an impromptu speech is brief. It can be as brief as a word or a sentence. It can also have a few sentences, depending on the situation and the length of the speech. You must be creative with this. The introduction of the speech should create an orientation. It should let your audience know what you are going to talk about for the time that you will be speaking. It is the curtain coming up for your speech.

Where you can, start with an attention-getter, just like with a regular speech, this helps to draw in and capture your audience's attention. It could be a quote, a statistic, a question, a one-liner joke, etcetera, all of which should be relevant to the content of your speech and must contribute to the message you are trying to share. Please note that you have to be creative in using attention getter for impromptu speeches.

The introduction can also contain a brief preview of the main points of the speech. It is especially possible for Impromptu speeches that have been "rehearsed." I will explain what I mean by "rehearsed" in a later chapter. I will show you why an impromptu speech is not always impromptu.

But remember, previewing your main point is not always necessary for an impromptu speech. The absence of a preview does not in any way harm the logical flow of your points.

The Body

The body, which should be the lengthiest part of the speech, adds flesh and substance to the speech. In the body, you will state your claims or your main points. These points give meaning to your speech.

The main points of the speech must not stand in isolation; they must have support(s). This is because the points most times are claims or strong assertions. For example, your point on a speech on "The Effect Massive Open Online Courses (MOOC) on traditional University" could be that MOOC's can see the eventual death of the traditional university, although this is a broad point. You cannot make such a claim and leave it to stand alone. To drive this point home, you must provide adequate support. Support, in this case, could be that since MOOC's started becoming prominent globally, most universities have seen a sharp decline in the amount of student application to a brick and mortar classroom. Adding this support, give your listeners a reason to want to agree with the main point that MOOC's can see the eventual death of the traditional university.

The number of supports attached to the main point depends on how much you are willing to reinforce your position or how much evidence you have at your disposal to support your claim or maybe the format of impromptu you wish to employ. It is okay to have three supports for a one-point impromptu, two supports each for a two-point impromptu, and at least one support each for a three-point impromptu speech format.

The Conclusion

In the conclusion of your speech, you must find a concise and logical way to end your speech. The conclusion should also be brief, just like the introduction. This part of the speech is equally as important as the introduction of the speech. The conclusion may also restate your statement in the introduction and review the points in the body. Although this is dependent on how much time you have to speak.

In rhetoric, a speech is sometimes considered to be cyclical and not linear. This means that the conclusion should, in a sense, connect back to the introduction. Arranging your impromptu speech in this manner creates a more integrated structure and ultimately gives your speech a more substantial impact.

Impromptu Speech Formats

The above speech components are arranged in three basic formats. These formats are predominantly used in the delivery of impromptu speeches. The formats are shown below. Because I want you to understand and appreciate these structures, practical and real-life examples from different events are included to give a vivid illustration of how they work and, most importantly, how you can apply them.

One Point Format:

A one-point impromptu speech format contains an introduction and just one main point. This main point should have at most three supports. After the main point, comes the conclusion.

I. Introduction
II. Main point
  A. Support #1
  B. Support #2
  C. Support #3
III. Conclusion

Example:
This is a real-life example from CNN's Christiane Amanpour's interview with the former Saudi Minister of Foreign Affairs, Adel Al-Jubeir, on the war in Syria and President Bashar Assad's position.

Christiane: What is your assessment of the strength of Bashar al-Assad now, given the three and half months of Russian airstrikes that have supported him?

Adel:
Introduction: I believe Bashar al-Assad is weak and does not have a future in Syria.
Main point: Bashar al-Assad butchered, massacred and killed his people, men, women and children. And his military couldn't save him, **(Support #1)** so he prevailed upon the Iranians to come and support him, who sent their Quds Forces and the Revolutionary Guards and they, in turn, couldn't save him.
(Support #2) So Iran and Bashar al-Assad mobilized Hezbollah, Shia militias from Iraq, Pakistan, Afghanistan. And they, in turn, couldn't save him. **(Support #3)** And now we have Russia going into Syria in support of Bashar al-Assad. And they will not be able to save him.
Conclusion: The man who is responsible for the murder of 300,000-plus people, the displacement of 12 million people, the destruction of a country, is a man with absolutely no future in this country.

Two Point Format:
The two-point impromptu speech format contains an introduction, two main points, and a conclusion. Each of these main points should have at most two supports to drive home the points.

I. Introduction
II. First main point
  A. Support #1
  B. Support #2
III. Second main point
  A. Support #1
  B. Support #2
IV. Conclusion

Example:
In India, a young female medical student was gang-raped and brutalized on a bus in New Delhi and died from her injuries. The event was captured in the documentary "India's Daughter." Again, CNN's Christiane Amanpour interviews the director of this documentary, Leslee Udwin, on her perspective on the issue. Below is an excerpt as it fits a two-point impromptu speech format.

Christiane: How does this change, I mean, your film, the outrage that poured out onto the streets after she was gang-raped three years ago. It seems like it's all there for a little moment and then it gets swept away again. Is there a way, is there a big enough group of people in India who are willing to make this real change?

Leslee:
Introduction: No. There isn't a big enough group of people anywhere in the world. But the perspective, the insights I gleaned on this journey was so seemingly blindingly clear to me. They led to the perspective of what I know to be the solution, and what I would venture to say is the only solution.

Main point #1: What we are dealing with here is mindset. **(Support #1)** The rape, the rapist, this isn't the disease. They are but the symptom of the disease, as is trafficking, as is beheading people. The disease is a mindset that accords no value to another human being. **(Support #2)** A mindset that has not been thought and practiced in empathy in seeing the world from another human being's point of view. It's violation of human rights, whether those human rights are being violated on a racial, religious, or gender basis.

Main point #2: So how do we change mindset? There is only one way, education. **(Support #1)** And when I came to examine what it is, we are teaching children of the world. I realized forcibly we are teaching them numeracy and literacy. We are totally neglecting their holistic moral education, teaching them respect, breaking down gender stereotypes, teaching them ethics and empathy. **(Support #2)** And I am actually spearheading a global education initiative, which I am advising the UN human rights office on which I know will change the world. And we have extraordinary supporters, for the film and the initiative; Meryl Streep, Eric Thompson.

Conclusion: We are starting a theatrical campaign with the film now which points out the problem and launching this education campaign which is the solution.4

Three-Point Format:
The three-point impromptu speech format contains an introduction, three main points, and a conclusion. In this case, each main point has one support attached to it.

I. Introduction
II. First main point
  A. Support
III. Second main point
  A. Support
IV. Third main point
  A. Support
V. Conclusion

Example:

In one of my classes on public speaking, I made each participant write out a topic on a piece of paper and then fold it. And all the topics placed in a basket and mixed. I had each participant pick paper from the basket. A lady picked the paper with the word "diamond." This was how she dealt with the topic.

Introduction: What other jewelry would you price above that made with Diamonds? Diamonds, as we know them, are precious stones, stones of estimable value. There is no other gemstone that we could liken to the heart of a good person but a diamond.

Main Point #1 Men with diamond hearts gave freedom to several faces of humanity, freedom that was desperately sought after. **(Support)**The diamond heart of Martin Luther King emancipated the black race from years of slavery and oppression. It was Nelson Mandela that liberated the people of South Africa from the stronghold of apartheid that plagued them for years. This was a man with a diamond heart.

Main Point #2 The diamond hearts of some good people have also made the world a beautiful place to live in. They have made life easier. They saw the needs of humanity and made an effort to meet those needs. **(Support)** Mark Zuckerberg, for example, is diamond indeed, creating a platform for global connectivity. Steve Jobs, Elon Musk are just a few amongst many.

Main Point #3 What about those people who are passionate about sharing knowledge? They are diamonds. **(Support)** Our teachers, our professors, and even the instructor of this class, Mr. Solomon, they are all diamonds.

Conclusion: So, you can see that diamonds go beyond just that precious stone; they reflect in the hearts and minds of humans. They are all around us.

What You Need to Know About These Formats

Outlining an impromptu speech to conform to a rubric gives you a clearer insight into the structure of an organized impromptu speech and makes you appreciate the whole process. The above are the three basic formats that are applied as templates for the effective and logical delivery of impromptu speeches. However, your impromptu speech mustn't always fit with the above structures. You can have a speech with one main point and one support, or two main points and one support each. The key takeaway is to make a point and support the point you make, also to have the flow of an introduction, a body, and a conclusion.

The important thing is that having a structure for impromptu speeches create an elemental framework that is required for a logical outline and progression of a speech. Also note that lengthier speeches conform to the basic structure of an introduction, a body, and a conclusion, but in this case, a more elaborate introduction, body and conclusion and sometimes more points to discuss.

With this as a mental backdrop, you should have a clear picture of how to arrange your thought logically and coherently for any kind of impromptu speech. Whether you are required to answer a question, or you are at an interview, or maybe you are called upon to give an impromptu toast or even stand-in for a speaker that is absent. This is a great tool that serves as a template for success.

For good measure, I have an additional example. In this example, former US President Barack Obama spoke with the BBC ahead of his trip to East Africa. Below is an excerpt from the transcript of Editor Jon Sopel's conversation with the US president.

Jon Sopel: Mr. President, you're about to fly to Kenya to your ancestral home. Given the al-Shabaab attacks on the West Gate mall and Garissa University, I'm sure your secret service could've suggested other countries for you to visit. But you wanted to go to Kenya.

President Barack Obama: Well, I think it is important first of all that the president of the United States underscores our commitment to partnering with countries around the world, even though we're not intimidated by terrorist organizations. Second, the counterterrorism co-operation between the United States and Kenya - and Uganda and other countries - in East Africa - is very strong.

And part of the subject of the visit is to continue to strengthen those ties to make them more effective. Third, as I wind down my presidency, I've already had a number of visits to Africa. But this gives me an opportunity to focus on a region that I have not been visiting as president, and I'm also going to have the opportunity to talk to the African Union.

So I'll be the first US president to not only visit Kenya and Ethiopia but also to address the continent as a whole, building off the African summit that we did here which was historic and has, I think, deepened the kinds of already strong relationships that we have across the continent.

The Privilege of a Rubric

An excellent impromptu speech could either be to inform, persuade, or to entertain an audience. A decent delivery from a good speaker is not just another talk or speech without any form or order. It is structured, just like any good speech should have a structure. This skeletal representation of an impromptu speech is of enormous benefit for anyone who desires to be a good speaker, for all they need to do is wrap their thoughts around this structure to make it coherent and logical. You must begin to appreciate by now the relevance of having a structure in a speech. You have seen so far how you can establish coherence and how it can make a speech interesting to listen to, creating a logical pattern in the mind of listeners.

In the next chapter, we shall look at strategies that you can use to deliver impromptu speeches for maximum impact.

CHAPTER FOUR

Strategies for Success

What's the use of running if you are not on the right road?
-German proverb

Just like planning is a prerequisite to achieving success, having a strategy that is suited for different kinds of topics is necessary for delivering an organized, logical, and impactful impromptu speech. Depending on the topic you have before you, all you need to do is select from your repertoire of strategies. You could marshal the strategy that is most effective to layout and address the subject at hand. Strategies are important. Remember, if you don't know where you are going, any road will get you there.

Strategies are essential for impromptu speeches, contrary to what you may think. If you don't take out time to look deep into the nature and pattern of impromptu speeches, you might think they don't have a structure or are not strategic. Although with practice, the effective use of strategies for different topics becomes second nature. That is why those that are proficient at delivering impromptu speeches make it look effortless and ordinary. But the truth is that giving an organized presentation doesn't just happen out of the blues; it takes practice; it takes lots of exposure to impromptu speaking situations. If you look closely at these individuals, you will observe that there are several common patterns in the way they deliver these short speeches. They effectively deploy strategies to achieve such a superior level of thought and a compelling presentation.

You must understand that strategies are available, not only to help you think quickly on your feet but also to make your speech persuasive and to prevent you from rambling, which is bound to happen when there is no clear path for presenting your thoughts. So, having a strategy is also like having a rubric or like following a format, as I discussed in an earlier chapter.

In this chapter, we are going to go further beyond just having a structure, we are going to address the best ways to layout your thoughts around a strategy.

Before looking at conventional strategies, I think one important thing to always do is to anticipate the possibility of presenting an impromptu speech.

First, Be on the Defensive
The more your responsibilities increase, the more likely you will be faced with impromptu speaking situations. And as such, it is essential to anticipate such situations. For example, if you are attending a function where you are popular among the attendees, just ponder over topics that would be relevant to that audience and the possibility that you would be called upon to speak. Or if you are attending an engagement party of a close friend, think of the possibility of speaking or sharing your thoughts about your friend with the audience, because there is a reasonable chance that you might be asked to do so. Also, if for example, your immediate superior or team member at work is scheduled to speak at a meeting, it is okay to think around the subject of discussion, because you might find yourself speaking.

As you approach such events, try to be proactive, carry out some mental exercises, try to think about the possible subjects of discussion, also think of what subject they might ask you to talk about if it comes down to that. You will be surprised how these thoughts will help you improve your delivery when you find yourself in the spotlight. This is what I refer to as a defensive mechanism. You must be on the lookout.

Be Quick to Apply a Strategy
Just imagine that you have an assignment to move from point A to point B with the help of a map, but when you were ready

to start your journey, you picked up the wrong map, let's say a map that takes you from A to C. If you ignorantly make a move with that wrong map, you will leave your original position A, but it will not get you to your desired destination, which is B.

In like manner, when you have a subject to speak about, you should ensure that the strategy you choose is suitable for the subject that you need to address. Strategies for impromptu speeches are not one size fits all. The suitability of a strategy depends on the subject you are responding to or speaking about. There are several ways that we can use to categorize impromptu speech topics. For example, you can place topics in groups like famous people, places, current events, words (conceptual/abstract and operational/objects and things), proverbs, quotations, and phrases. For each category, you should use the most suitable impromptu speech strategy to address them.

These strategies are templates for delivering excellent impromptu speeches. Think of strategy and structure as molds. For the mold to produce a shape, you have to pour the content into it. In this case, your knowledge is where you draw your material from, to fit or align with the mold. I will discuss four of these strategies in this chapter.

Past, Present, and Future
It is best to discuss certain topics in chronological order. With the past, present, and future strategy, you will need to reflect on the past, stating what happened, then go ahead to discuss what is happening in the present, and finally rounding up with what could happen in the future. This strategy works well for several types of questions and impromptu topics on events and places, etc.

When you approach a subject using the past, present, and future framework, it does an excellent job of creating a broad but linear perspective on the subject. With this structure, you will be able to address the history of that event and how it connects with the current state of things and, ultimately, what is possible in the future.

But remember, the use of this approach in speaking about events depends on the angle from which you intend to address the subject. You could also use other methods to address a different concern relating to the event.

Now let us look at some examples of how you can structure an impromptu speech to conform to this framework.

Example 1
What gets you excited about life?

I believe that life is a journey that has several journeys contained in it, and excitement depends on the journey that you are on.

For example, I remember as a child, the one thing that gets me overwhelmingly excited was Christmas and Santa Claus. At that time, I would not trade the joy and happiness that came with the season for anything else in the world. But when I became a teenager, Christmas was less exciting, and the thought of getting into college was exhilarating, I could not wait to get in. Now, as a full-blown adult, what gets me excited is the prospect of creating a successful business, and it feels like nothing else matters. However, looking at the future, it is hard to tell what I will be excited about.

And so, I believe that excitement in life depends largely on time and season.

Example 2
What do you know about Dubai?

Dubai is one of the fastest-growing cities in the world. It is a city that has become a popular travel/tourist destination in the world. The fact is that the city has not always been like this. The Dubai we know and appreciate today passed through a series of developmental stages.

In its early years, Dubai was successful but on a regular scale. The region at that time was known for fishing, pearling, and sea trade. The amount of trading increased significantly, and

Dubai ultimately became a prosperous port. This strengthened its position as a major trading and re-export hub.

But today's Dubai city was birthed after the discovery of oil in 1966. The increase in revenue that resulted from the discovery brought about massive infrastructural development. They built hospitals, schools, functional road networks, modern telecommunication networks, among other things. This development was further increased when the decision was made to diversify from an oil-reliant economy to one that is service and tourism-oriented. As a result, Dubai currently has several infrastructural records, the world's tallest tower, the world's largest shopping mall, the world's tallest hotel, and several others.

I think the world is yet to see the last of Dubai's growth and innovation. The city currently houses 25% of the world's crane because of the heavy construction taking place in multiple on-going projects, which would further strengthen the country's relevance on the global stage.

Dubai is the fastest-growing city and will continue to enjoy global attention for a very long time.

Example 3
What are your thoughts on the Iraq war?

When I think of the war in Iraq, I can't help but think of, firstly, a country that has been in war since the 1920's, and secondly, the number of lives that are lost in these wars.

The Republic of Iraq has always been a troubled region, looking back from the great Iraq revolution in 1920. The painful things about these wars are the number of lives that are lost. According to the Opinion Research Business Survey on Iraq war casualties, there were over 1,033,000 deaths between 2003 and 2007.

The country is currently in an ongoing insurgency that began in 2017, and lives are being lost.

The sad truth is that no one can boldly guarantee a peaceful Iraq in the future as several violent religious sects spring up from every corner in that region.

Looking at the historical facts of the war in Iraq, one thing is always constant, as in every other war, lives are lost.

The three examples above are good illustrations of impromptu speeches that conform to the past, present, and future model. Also, all three speeches have the basic structure of a speech; that is, they all have an introduction, a body, and a conclusion. We discussed this subject in the previous chapter.

I specifically added examples 2 and 3 not just because they are good examples of a speech with the past, present, and future model, but because of the amount of information that they have. In the second example, there is good information on the history of Dubai with some statistics. Also, for the third example, there are relevant information and statistics. What this means is that both the second and third speaker have a good knowledge of the subject. And to be able to cite statistics and provide such detail, one must not only be knowledgeable, but must also have a good memory. That is why a chapter of this book is on memory.

The past, present, and future strategy help the audience broaden their understanding of a subject on a time scale.

Cause, Effect, and Remedy

You can address several topics using the cause, effect, and remedy approach. But this strategy is most applicable to problem-related subjects. For example, anxiety, abortion, racism, cancer, and conflict are some of the topics that I consider problem-related. This strategy creates a panoramic view of the subject matter, addressing it from three significant angles. See the example below.

Example
Gun violence in America

Gun violence has become a plague in American society. As

you know, the number of deaths by guns in America stands far apart from other developed nations.

Many would argue that exposure to violent games and movies, easy access to guns, a decline in parenting and family values, and early release of violent offenders are the major causes of this hideous crime. To this, I can't agree more.

For example, the easier it is for everybody and anybody to have a gun, the higher the chances of mass shootings and suicides. Also, the figures have shown painfully that these shootings are mostly perpetrated by teenagers, a group that is more likely to be influenced by violent games and videos.

But the question that we find ourselves always asking is, how can this societal plague be stopped? I believe the government should pass strict and sensible gun laws to ensure gun control. Parents should do a better job at parenting to create rich and enduring family values.

It has always been my desire to see an America that is free from gun violence. An America with one voice; an America united to stamp-out this societal ill.

Please note that the above example is not for you to agree or disagree with; it is meant to show you how to frame your thoughts using cause, effect, and remedy strategy.

PREP Method

The PREP method is a fundamental and excellent strategy for speaking. It is best to use this framework when you have just one central idea or main point to emphasize. PREP is an acronym that stands for:

P- Point
R- Reason
E- Example
P- Point

I see this method as a very balanced approach in handling an impromptu topic. Because psychologically, by giving a reason for your point, you appeal to your audience's left brains. When you support this with an example, you appeal to their right emotional brains. And when you go over the point again at the end, you create a stronger impression of your claim.

Example:
Point: Florida is an exceedingly pleasing destination for a vacation.
Reason: There are numerous beautiful tourist sites in the state, like the Walt Disney World Resort, Everglades National Park, Universal Studios, and many others.
Example: I was there on vacation with my family two years ago, and our experience still has a strong impression on every one of us.
Point: Florida is always my first recommendation for anyone looking to go on a vacation.

Remember, you should consider this strategy mostly when you have one idea to stress upon.

Before, the Event, the Result
This strategy allows you to present your idea in chronological order, almost like the past, present, and future strategy. When asked to describe a situation, you could use this strategy. It is also a good template that can help you organize your ideas.

Just as the name implies, with this strategy, you discuss whatever happened before the subject, then you go ahead to address what is happening with the subject and then the possible outcome of the current actions. The subject, in this case, could be anything from discussing a business strategy, a global pandemic, improving a relationship, etc.

The Strategy When You Don't Have a Strategy.
There are times when you can't think of a strategy. Some other times you might not have a direct answer to a question, or maybe the question is one that is difficult to answer. These moments do happen, even in times when you think that you

are prepared. What do you do in these moments? How do you shine in these moments?

You Can Always Count on Stories

Stories are powerful. They are an excellent tool to persuade or instruct an audience. A story is one of the most powerful ways to engage and connect with an audience. They create pictures in the mind of your audience, and a story by itself can be a complete and perfect answer to a question.

If you find yourself in a position where you cannot think of a strategy, or perhaps a question seems to be too difficult to answer directly, you can just tell a story. When a story is compelling and well delivered, it not only engages the audience in that moment, it also stays in their minds long after you are done talking. That means you don't just tell stories because you don't have anything to say; in fact, they are the most powerful support within a speech structure. So, use well-constructed stories to pass across your message as much as you can.

One of the challenges with stories is that they are sometimes difficult to recall when speaking impromptu. This is where personal story mining comes in. Personal story mining is when you pull out stories from your past and present, write them down, and then refine them in a way that is compelling for conversations, impromptu speeches, and prepared speeches. This could include stories of your personal life experiences, events you witnessed, the experiences of people you know, etc.

You might think you don't have stories to tell until you start mining. I have worked with clients who thought they had no stories to tell but were surprised at how many compelling stories they were able to recall and refine. In the "Work it out" session at the end of this book, there is a worksheet to help you out with the first stage of the personal story mining process.

The Principle of The First Thought

Sometimes, the reason why we are not able to answer a question is because of the internal dialogue that takes place in

47

our minds when we hear a question. We think about things like, "I don't know if I can answer this question." "What are people going to say if I am not articulate?" "This was not the question I was expecting." etc.

The principle of the first thought says that once you hear a question, begin with the first thought that comes to your mind. This principle helps you quiet the noise and cuts out the internal dialogue going on in your mind. But the question, however, is what do you do after you've said the first line of what you have in mind? What comes next?

Firstly, you cannot take back what you've said. Once the words are uttered, you have to go on from there. Hopefully, your first thought is not a crazy one.

Secondly, there is good news; you can think as you speak. When you start to speak, your brain generates fresh ideas that connect with your initial thought or ideas. Several people speak slowly, and use a lot of pauses, just so they can have the time to think as they speak.

Choose What to Answer

Who says you must answer the question? The truth is that you can decide to go in a different direction with your answer. We see this all the time on TV when an interviewee keeps going around a question. Sometimes these individuals even get a standing ovation for a response that is not in any way connected to the question that was asked. This is common with politicians.

There are several things you could do if a question doesn't sit well with you. Firstly, you can disagree with the question and state what you believe. Secondly, you can answer part of the question. Thirdly, you can change the direction of the question.

Think of These Strategies

Generally, when I think of strategies, I think of a path to success. I think of the fulfillment of knowing exactly where you are going. I think of the absence of confusion. The above strategies as they exist for speaking allows you to wrap your response to a topic around simple but effective templates, or to lay those thoughts and points nicely on the appropriate framework. Remember that your overarching goal is for your speech to be coherent, logical, meaningful, and impactful to your audience. Knowing and employing these strategies make this very easy to accomplish. If you practice using these strategies, you will find out how easy it will be to respond to issues and speak intelligently without prior notice or preparation.

CHAPTER FIVE

Language, a Basic Unit

Language is power, life, and the instrument of culture, the instrument of domination and liberation.
-Angela Carter

The Potency of Language

I must start by saying language is powerful. It is very difficult to imagine a world without language. It is the most potent tool for human communication. You have a better understanding of the world around you because of language. As a child, you learned a language to read, write, and speak. After you had mastered enough of your language, you were able to communicate with relative ease.

Language is culturally transmitted. You learn a language of communication from those around you. For most of us, this means that we may first learn our manner of communication from our parents, but as we grow older, other family members, friends, educators, and even the media impact our vocabularies and our choices regarding what words we use and how we use them.

The knowledge we have of the world around us is possible because of our experiences and the words we use to describe them. This chapter and the next focus on the power and beauty of language and how competent speakers harness language to deliver persuasive speeches both long and short.

Why Is Language Important?

Pause for a moment and then take a minute to observe your environment. Look at the things you have around you. How would you communicate the state and nature of what you see around you to an audience, in a way that they have a very good picture of what your environment looks like? According to Dale Carnegie "Your purpose is to make your audience see what you saw, hear what you heard, feel what you felt. Relevant details, couched in concrete, colorful language, is the best way to recreate the incident as it happened and to picture it for the audience." No matter what you are describing, this statement should give you a good insight into the effect of good use of language and how you can make it work for you. A vivid language construction reflects and maintains your social realities. It shapes our understanding.

You must understand that it is your use of language that determines how powerful your speech would be. Your communication must be effective to ensure that your ideas are transmitted and received just exactly as you want them to be received and that they are memorable. Also, when you are speaking, you should always have your audience at the back of your mind. Consider how their level of understanding and their use of language differs from yours. If how they translate an idea is different from yours, you must try to bridge the gap. You must also know that your audience makes certain assumptions of you based on the kind of language that you use.

The question is, why is this important in impromptu speeches? No matter what you are responding to, no matter the question that you are answering, your goal is to pass across a clear and persuasive message to your audience. To make this possible, you need to use the right words and use them in a way that not only accurately reflect your thoughts and feelings but also make your audience feel how you want them to feel. This is only possible when you use the right words.

The Use of Language in Speeches
When you think of Dr. Martin Luther King Jnr, you remember a man that was an outstanding speaker. He was a master in the use of persuasive language. He understood the power of communication, and he used it in a way that moved his

audience. His eloquence still resounds even in this generation and definitely in generations to come. Many other great speakers in history moved their audience to action just by the way and manner they spoke. Language is what makes up oral communication. It is the blood that gives life and meaning to spoken communication. When the blood is contaminated, the whole body suffers. So, you should always use a language that clearly expresses the thoughts and ideas you want your audience to receive and also for your words to have maximum impact. Consider the following points when using language.

Construct Clear and Vivid Messages

Language is a non-concrete phenomenon; meanings exist in our understanding. You must, therefore, enhance understanding by constructing your messages most clearly for the benefit of anyone who is listening. For example, if you're telling a story and you use the word "car," be sure to specify the type of car that you want to convey to your audience. You might have a luxury Rolls-Royce Phantom in mind, while your audience might be thinking of a regular car, maybe a Honda SUV. A lack of clarity makes your audience spend time and mental energy, trying to imagine the kind of car that fits with your story. This can only happen when you are not clear about your message. When you fail to use vivid language, you send a weak and sometimes different message from what you intend your audience to perceive. You may think it makes little difference, but at the end of the day, it contributes to how persuasive your message will be. So, when speaking, like in our example, be sure to use a description that is easy to visualize, like "Rolls Royce Phantom" over the ambiguous term "car."

Here is another example: if you say, "the weather condition was bad," the statement lacks enough details to help the listener visualize what the weather was like. Stating the temperature, the humidity, or other weather indicators would create a clear message with a more substantial impact on your audience.

Use Simple Language

We are in a time where simplicity with words is the trend. Gone are the days when inflated words make you gain influence. So, I find it amusing when people use big words where simple and clear words can do the job. If your goal is not to confuse your audience but to pass a clear message across that you want them to understand, then you must keep your language as simple as possible. For example, instead of saying:

"The undue favoritism of the instructor left the learners discombobulated."

Be kind enough to say:

"Because the instructor treated some students better than others, they felt cheated."

Don't be one of the people whom George Carlin referred to when he described language as a tool for concealing the truth. Always remember not to use an inflated language when you intend to keep your message simple and clear.

Stay Close to Your Audience

Nelson Mandela once said that if you talk to a man in a language he understands, it goes to his head. But when you speak to him in his language, it goes to his heart.

As a people, community, culture, and group or as individuals, we sometimes decide the words we use to define things. And so, as a speaker, you must think very carefully about the language of your audience when speaking. If you are speaking to a specialized audience, ensure that you communicate in their language. On the other hand, when you are speaking to a lay audience, you must speak in a way they would understand. When you do this, your audience will receive your message with open hearts and minds.

Avoid Jargon

Jargon is the "specialized language" used by a group or profession to communicate ideas or concepts that are familiar to that group. It is wrong to use jargon for an audience that cannot relate to what you are saying. When you avoid using jargon, it helps your audience get a better understanding of what you are saying. For example, if you are a lawyer and you are speaking to a group of lawyers, using legal jargon will help establish your credibility with that audience. But when speaking to a general audience and you use legal terms, it might distort the message you are trying to pass across to that audience. If you must use jargon while speaking to a general audience, make sure you define your terms.

Avoid Slang

Slang are very casual words or expressions that are sometimes playful replacements for standard ones and are considered unsuitable in a formal setting or polite conversations. Slang may be a poor choice for a speaker because some members of your audience may not be familiar with the slang term you use. Depending on the audience and the situation, you must try to avoid using slang to prevent any form of confusion. However, if you are speaking to an audience that you believe will understand your slang, you may choose to include it. Otherwise, do not use slang, or you may confuse your audience.

Using slang when speaking may communicate negative ideas about you to your audience.

Use Personalized Language

Humans are naturally more interested in themselves than others. For this simple reason, to grab the attention of your audience when speaking, ensure to use personalized language. Instead of saying, "One must avoid," say, "You must avoid." By using language that directly connects your topic to the audience, you increase the chances of getting them to listen and to be persuaded that your subject matter is serious and valuable to them. Using words like "us," "you," and "we" can be a subtle way to get your audience to pay attention to what you are saying. Most people are interested in things that they believe will impact their lives directly—make those connections clear to your audience by using personalized language.

Avoid Incorrect Grammar

Incorrect grammar can get into your speech in several ways. The three most common ways are through basic grammatical errors, mispronunciations, and colloquialisms.

For example, the sentence "He get too excited when he scores in a football match" is grammatically incorrect. This sentence is wrong because the verbs "get" and "score" are plural verbs which ought not to be as the subject "he" is singular. The correct sentence is, "He gets too excited when he scores in a football match."

Mispronunciations are also very common in speeches, especially if English is not a speaker's first language. But making pronunciation mistakes, when the words are very common, especially as perceived by the general public, could affect your credibility.

Colloquialisms are words or phrases that might be used in casual conversations but are inappropriate in formal settings. "I ain't" in place of "I am not" is a good example.

I can imagine what you are thinking, "this is ridiculous!" "How does this matter?" I understand your concern, especially in this day and age when the explosion of social media and the ultimate amplification of numerous ideologies have blurred the line between right and wrong, and it seems like the English language is evolving. Our choice of words in conversations is also changing. Several terms are gradually sliding into our daily conversations, and there is no telling how they would influence our language over time. So, it is not always easy to conform to these proper standards in these times. However, what I am trying to make you do is to prevent anything that distracts the mind of your listeners from your message. But my final advice on this would be for you to use your best judgment with careful consideration of your audience.

Transition Words and Phrases

Transition words or phrases are an essential part of language use and are crucial in conversations and speeches. They also help a speaker move from one point to the next. Remember, your goal for an impromptu speech is to convey an idea or information with clarity. You need transitions in your speech to help you achieve this goal. Using transitions effectively in your speeches does the following:

1. Transitions enhance logical organization and clarity of your message, and they also improve the connection between thoughts. They indicate the relationship between ideas within your message.
2. Transitions tell listeners what to do with the information you present to them, especially how to think about, organize, and react to the message you are sharing.
3. A speaker uses transition words and phrases to recall for the listener that which has already been said, and to help them anticipate that which is about to follow.
4. Transition words and phrases can create powerful links between ideas in your speech.

Before using a transitional word in your speech, be sure you understand its meaning and how to use it. Also, be sure that it is the right match for the message you wish to pass across.

Transition words and phrases play several roles in a speech. You need to understand these roles for easy applicability in all forms of conversations and presentations. The following are some transition statements and the role they play in a speech.

Transition to Indicate Addition

Equally, important, likewise also, Besides, by the same token, and, furthermore, similarly,   in addition, again, further, at the same time, what is more, as well as, moreover

Example:
I think I am the most suitable for this position because I have

a master's degree in business administration as well as ten years' managerial experience.

Transition to Indicate Time
In the meantime, afterward, secondly, next, as long as, after a while, lately, then, thereafter, until, shortly, after, in the future, before, at last, in the past, meanwhile, as soon as, simultaneously, presently, ultimately, formerly, so far, subsequently, first, Later, earlier, finally.

Example:
I am heading to the restaurant to have lunch; then, I will branch by the store to get groceries.

Transition to Indicate Comparison
Similarly, likewise, in like manner, at the same time, in the same way, by the same token, also, in comparison, in turn.

Example:
He oversees five major departments in the company and, at the same time, a pastor in his local church.

Transition to Indicate Contrast
But at the same time, regardless, nevertheless, for all that, despite, in contrast, on the other hand, however, though, conversely, but, in spite of, even so, nonetheless, yet, whereas, notwithstanding, even though, on the contrary, still.

Example:
She prepared very hard for the test, yet her grades were very low.

Transition to Indicate Cause or effect
For this purpose, as a consequence, hence, then, as a result, in short, to this end, Thereupon, because, therefore, accordingly.

Example:
The manager ignored the recommendation of the sales executive, and as a result, they lost the contract to competition.

Transition to Indicate Example
Such as, for instance, specifically, in particular, an illustration of, namely, to demonstrate, to illustrate, even, for example.

Example:
Over the last five years, global temperature has risen dramatically, with greater impact in regions such as the Middle East and Asia.

Transition to indicate Explanation
Indeed, in other words, put another way, in fact, simply stated.

Example:
I had a very nice time on my vacation in Australia. In fact, I visited every major tourist site.

Transition to Indicate Concession
Even though, of course, after all, at the same time, it is true, actually.

Example:
I was not entirely happy with the way the movie ended, even though I agree that it was a technically masterful production.

Transition to Indicate Place or direction
Above, over, there, opposite to, below, beneath, to the east, nearby, farther on, elsewhere, beyond, around, adjacent to, to the left, on the other side, next to.

Example:
He sat next to his colleague at the seminar, but they could not indulge in their regular chat because on the other side of the room was the MD, who was constantly looking at their direction.

Transition to Indicate Conclusion

In essence, in brief, as has been indicated, as has been said, in summary, altogether, to sum up, all in all, on the whole, in retrospect, in other words, in simpler terms, in conclusion, to summarize, finally.

Example:
Paul had drafted his plans, completed a comprehensive market research, raised sufficient capital; altogether, he was ready for business.

Don't Despise Good Use of Language

Language is the brick and mortar in communication. It is the blood that keeps communication alive. It is exciting to know that when you speak, your message is clear, direct, and well-received by an audience. This is basically what communication is all about. You must take note of this because it is a crucial component of effective speaking. To get a clearer understanding of the importance of language, make a conscious effort to observe and study how it functions within a speech, and how audiences react to it. When you become a master in this area, your impromptu speeches will be more persuasive.

CHAPTER SIX

The Beauty of Style

To understand language styles, think of how fashion enhances human outlook
-Solomon Asine

Typically, this chapter should be a part of the chapter on language, but I deliberately made it a separate chapter, firstly, to decongest the chapter on language and secondly, because of how special and important I believe styles (or stylistic devices) are in the art of speaking. Stylistic devices are still a sub-categorization of language; there is no doubt about that. But in this chapter, you will see the beauty that styles bring into a speech, how it adds power to a message. When you understand how they function and how they can set your speech apart, you will realize how important they are.

What Are Styles?

I would say that styles are the beauty of language. They adorn a language. Styles give a special effect to the words you use when speaking, and it makes them sufficiently distinctive. They are a unique language technique that helps a listener see things differently. They make your speech enjoyable.

Stylistic devices play a significant role in speeches. A speaker can use styles to intensify the emotional emphasis that a piece of information conveys. They can be used to express or stir up a desired feeling in the listener or evoke imaginations by creating images with words. The primary purpose of style is to increase the effectiveness, clarity, and impact of a message.

The Beauty of Style

To help us create a foundation for understanding and uncovering the concept of style, please read the following transcript carefully.

"I have a message for our youth. I challenge them to have hope and not indulge in drug abuse. I told them that I was born in the slum and that nobody should be limited because they are born in the slum. I told them that even if they are from the slum, they still have the opportunity to make a decision. You can either break a window, or you can become a glazier. It is up to you to destroy the bricks in your neighborhood, or you can choose to become a brick mason and erect buildings. Don't break down doors, instead build them. I see defaced walls in the slums with vulgar words and symbols of destitution. What you should be doing is training yourselves to be painters and artists."

The above is a piece that I rewrote; an excerpt from Reverend Jesse Jackson's rainbow coalition speech at the 1984 Democratic National Convention. This edited content sends across the same message as the original text but without stylized language.

Now, read the original text as delivered by Reverend Jesse Jackson.

"I have a message for our youth. I challenge them to put hope in their brains and not dope in their veins. I told them that like Jesus, I, too, was born in the slum, and just because you're born in a slum does not mean the slum is born in you, and you can rise above it if your mind is made up. I told them in every slum there are two sides. When I see a broken window that's the slummy side. Train some youth to become a glazier; that is the sunny side. When I see a missing brick, that is the slummy side. Let that child in a union and become a brick mason and build; that is the sunny side. When I see a missing door, that is the slummy side. Train some youth to become a carpenter, that is the sunny side. When I see the vulgar words and hieroglyphics of destitution on the walls, that is the slummy side. Train some youth to be a painter and artist, that is the sunny side."

Why Use Style?

The original message, as seen above, is filled with stylized languages, and as a result, it sounds very different from my edited version. However, they both pass across a similar message. The question is, which version do you think is easier to remember? Which version do you think will most likely engage and uplift an audience? I would say the original version. I see style as a formula for eloquence. They help you communicate your meaning vividly, and with flair.

Also, as a matter of emphasis, it is important to remember that stylistic devices don't just make your message sound better; they also help to make your message memorable. If you take a closer look at the original transcript above, you will notice that there are patterns; also, pictures are painted with words to increase the chances that the message is committed to the memory of the listener. For example, the repetition of "slummy side" and "sunny side" creates a hook that takes hold of the listener's mind. This is one of many reasons why styles are essential in speaking.

There is so much to say about styles. There are hundreds of stylistic devices. Any book dedicated solely on rhetorical devices would amount to hundreds of pages. I do not intend to make this chapter an archive for stylistic devices; however, I am going to concentrate on a few of them here. The styles that I will be looking at are those that are common in speeches, those that you can use comfortably when speaking impromptu. Please note that other forms of style are also worthy of note.

Alliteration

Alliteration is a literary device that involves the repetition of the same consonant sound at the beginning of multiple words that are close to each other.

Alliteration brings the listener's attention to that particular area of your message and also increases emphasis on the words. It creates aural rhythm and helps the listener commit your message to memory.

Example 1:
"Somewhere at this moment, a child is being born. Let it be our cause to give that child a happy home, a healthy family, and a hopeful future."

Example 2:
"I have a dream that my four little children will one day live in a nation where they will not be judged by the color of their skin but by the content of their character."
— Martin Luther King, Jr.

Example 3:
"Have you forgotten you're facing the single finest fighting force ever assembled."
-- Dan Ackroyd (Dragnet, a 1987 film)

Anadiplosis
In this literary device, a word is used at the end of a sentence and then used again at the beginning of the next sentence. It is derived from the Greek word for "doubling up" or "folding up" as in a paper.

It can be used to demonstrate the relationship between things or events, and it is used most times to show cause and effect. The repetition of the words adds rhythm and cadence to a speaker's words. Anadiplosis often builds in intensity to a climax.

Example 1:
"They call for you: The general who became a slave; the slave who became a gladiator; the gladiator who defied an Emperor. A striking story."
- Commodus, (Gladiator, a 2000 film)

Example 2:
"And not only so, but we glory in tribulations also: knowing that tribulation worketh patience; and patience, experience;

and experience, hope: and hope maketh not ashamed..."
– Romans 5: 3-5 (The Bible, King James Version)

Example 3:
"Information is not knowledge; knowledge is not wisdom; wisdom is not truth; truth is not beauty; beauty is not love; love is not music, and music is the best."
– Frank Zappa

Anaphora
Anaphora is simply the repetition of a word or group of words at the beginning of two or more successive clauses or sentences.

Anaphora is one of the oldest literary devices, and it is derived from a Greek word that means "to bring back" or "to carry back."

The use of anaphora helps to emphasize keywords or ideas, and the fact that it involves repetition makes the lines memorable. It also gives rhythm to a speaker's words.

Example 1:
"We shall go on to the end, we shall fight in France, we shall fight on the seas and oceans, we shall fight with growing confidence and growing strength in the air, we shall defend our island whatever the cost may be, we shall fight on the beaches, we shall fight on the landing grounds, we shall fight in the fields and in the streets, we shall fight in the hills; we shall never surrender"- Winston Churchill

Example 2:
"To raise a happy, healthy, and hopeful child, it takes a family; it takes teachers; it takes clergy; it takes businesspeople; it takes community leaders; it takes those who protect our health and safety. It takes all of us."
–Hillary Clinton, 1996 DNC

Example 3:
"As you know, we've got the iPod, best music player in the world. We've got the iPod Nanos, brand new models, colors are back. We've got the amazing new iPod Shuffle."
— Steve Jobs, Macworld 2007 Keynote Address

Appositio
Appositio is a stylistic device in which words are placed side by side each other with one word describing or elaborating the other. It is the addition of an adjacent, coordinate, explanatory, or descriptive element.

These additions may not be required, but they are used for description or explanation. They also stress and emphasize a particular word or idea.

Example 1:
"And so, I ask you tonight, the people of Massachusetts, to think this through with me. In facing this decision, I seek your advice and opinion. In making it, I seek your prayers."
-- Edward M. Kennedy,

Example 2:
"John Fitzgerald Kennedy, a great and good President, a friend of all people of goodwill, a believer in the dignity and equality of all human beings, a fighter for justice, an apostle of peace, has been snatched from our midst by the bullet of an assassin."-Justice Earl Warren

Example 3:
"I, Barbara Jordan, am a keynote speaker."
- Barbara Jordan.

Asyndeton
Asyndeton is a literary device that intentionally omits conjunctions such as "and" "or" "for" and "but" from a series of related phrases or clauses. It is derived from the Greek word that means "unconnected."

Asyndeton adds rhythm and help in speeding up words. It leaves the impression that the list is not complete. For example, in the sentence "I can write, sing, dance." conveys the notion that I can do all three and maybe more. It leaves open the possibility for more options.

If, when speaking, you decide to use asyndeton to convey the impression that your list is incomplete, then ensure that your voice does not fall with the last word or phrase; instead, raise it higher or, at worse, keep it at the same level as the beginning.

Example 1:
"...we shall pay any price, bear any burden, meet any hardship, support any friend, oppose any foe to assure the survival and the success of liberty."
–John F. Kennedy

Example 2:
"For from within, out of the heart of man, come evil thoughts, sexual immorality, theft, murder, adultery, coveting, wickedness, deceit, sensuality, envy, slander, pride, foolishness. All these evil things come from within, and they defile a person."
- Mark 7:21-23 (The Bible, English Standard Version)

Example 3:
"Veni, vidi, vici" -Julius Caesar
This is an ecclesiastical Latin statement, translated into English as "I came, I saw, I conquered."

Epistrophe
Epistrophe, also known as Epiphora, is the repetition of the same word or words at the end of successive phrases, clauses, or sentences. It is derived from the Greek word, which means "return."

It is the counterpart of anaphora, which is the repetition words at the beginning of clauses. Epistrophe places serious emphasis on the last word or words in a phrase or sentence.

Example 1:
-Swearing oath in court - "I swear to tell the truth, the whole truth and nothing but the truth." –

Example 2:
"As long as the white man sent you to Korea, you bled. He sent you to Germany, you bled. He sent you to the south Pacific to fight the Japanese, you bled. You bleed for white people. But when it comes time to seeing your own churches being bombed and little black girls being murdered, you haven't got no blood."
- Malcolm X

Example 3:
"When I was a child, I spoke as a child, I understood as a child, I thought as a child."
— 1 Corinthians 13:11 (The Bible, King James Version)

Symploce
Symploce is also a repetitive style that combines the effect of anaphora and epistrophe. In this case, the first and last word or words in one phrase, clause, or sentence are repeated in two or more successive phrases, clauses, or sentences. It is derived from the Greek word, meaning "interweaving."

Like most other repetitive stylistic devices, Symploce draws the attention of the listener and create rhythm and emphasis, making the line more memorable.

Example 1:
"My brother need not be idealized, or enlarged in death beyond what he was in life, to be remembered simply as a good and decent man, who saw wrong and tried to right it, saw suffering and tried to heal it, saw war and tried to stop it."
–Ted Kennedy

Example 2:
"Much of what I say might sound bitter, but it's the truth. Much of what I say might sound like it's stirring up trouble, but it's the truth. Much of what I say might sound like it is hate, but it's the truth."
– Malcolm X

Example 3:
"Let us let our own children know that we will stand against the forces of fear. When there is talk of hatred, let us stand up and talk against it. When there is talk of violence, let us stand up and talk against it."
-- William Jefferson Clinton,

Polysyndeton

In this rhetorical style, several conjunctions like and, or, but, for, nor, so, etc. are used in close succession, even when they are contextually irrelevant. It is derived from a Greek word meaning "bound together with." It is also the structural opposite of asyndeton.

In polysyndeton, the repetition of the conjunctions gives extra power to the words. It also slows down the pace of the sentence with the addition of rhythm and cadence.
This Insertion of excessive conjunctions gives a feeling that you are building up your idea or thought.

Example 1:
"We must change that deleterious environment of the '80s, that environment which was characterized by greed and hatred and selfishness and mega-mergers and debt overhang..."- Barbara Jordan

Example 2:
"Let the white folks have their money and power and segregation and sarcasm and big houses and schools and lawns like carpets, and books, and mostly–mostly–let them have their whiteness." – Maya Angelou

Example 3:
"Oh, my piglets, we are the origins of war -- not history's forces, nor the times, nor justice, nor the lack of it, nor causes, nor religions, nor ideas, nor kinds of government -- not any other thing. We are the killers."
-        Katherine Hepburn (The Lion in Winter, a 1968 film)

Schesis Onomaton
Schesis onomaton is a figure of repetition in which series of words with synonymous expressions or words with somewhat close meaning occurs within the same sentence.

What schesis onomaton does is to stress and also bring attention to a particular word, statement, or idea.

Example 1:
"Because he's the hero Gotham deserves, but not the one it needs right now. So, we'll hunt him...because he can take it...because he's not our hero. He's a Silent Guardian, a Watchful Protector, a Dark Knight."
-- Gary Oldman (The Dark Knight, a 2008 film)

Example 2:
"A sinful nation, a people laden with iniquity, a seed of evildoers, children that are corrupters."
-- Isaiah 1:4, (The Bible, King James Version)

Example 3:
"Let there be no illusions about the difficulty of forming this kind of a national community. It's tough, difficult, not easy. But a spirit of harmony will survive in America only if each of us remembers that we share a common destiny."
-- Barbara Jordan, 1976 DNC Keynote Address

Rhetorical Styles and Impromptu Speeches
As I mentioned, stylistic devices adorn a speech, and in most cases, helps to commit your words and ideas to the memory of

your listeners. They are, therefore, important elements in speaking that you should not disregard.

Your ability to use these styles in impromptu speeches strengthens your credibility as a brilliant speaker. One might want to argue that these styles can only be used for prepared speeches, as it requires conscious effort to frame or put them together. I would argue otherwise. Anybody can use these styles easily and effectively in impromptu speeches. Anaphora, which is one of the most commonly used styles, is prevalent not just because it is easy to frame but because of how close people have come to it. They hear it often, they read it often, and so it comes to the mind quickly, more than any other style (based on my observation and research).

Your ability to use these styles when you speak impromptu depends on how much you expose yourself to them. The more you use them in prepared speeches and conversations, the more they become a part of you, and ultimately the easier you can bring them up when speaking impromptu.

CHAPTER SEVEN

Listen and Learn

Know how to listen, and you will profit even from those who talk badly.
-Plutarch

In his book, Leadership Gold, John C. Maxwell tells a story about two redneck hunters who were out in the woods. One of them falls to the ground, while they were walking. He doesn't seem to be breathing, and his eyes are rolled back in his head.

The other redneck starts to panic, then brings out his cell phone and calls 911.

He frantically blurts out to the operator, "My friend Bubba is dead! What can I do?"

The operator, trying to calm him down, says, "Take it easy. I can help. Just listen to me and follow my instructions. First, let's make sure he's dead."

There's a short pause, and then the operator hears a loud gunshot!

The redneck comes back on the line and says, "OK, now what?"

That is a funny story, but it is a good illustration of what could happen when we don't listen attentively and when we fail to listen for meaning.

Good speakers are good listeners. They understand the power and importance of active listening. Active listening is important for anybody who wants to learn and grow. However, as a speaker, it is also important to learn how to listen on a general sense and even when you speak. Yes, you can also listen when you speak. Although some people see speaking as a one-way process, believing that a speaker is just out to deliver a message to an audience. While this is true to some extent, it is not the entire story. When speaking, you get both non-verbal and verbal feedback from your audience. Your interpretation of these messages as a speaker should help you adjust your delivery to make your message have a maximum impact on the audience.

You could also find yourself in a situation where you need to respond impromptu to tough questions from an audience. Your ability to listen effectively in this situation is essential because it will give you a clear insight into what is said, and it will also help you provide a more accurate and meaningful response.

Developing your listening skills should be a priority if you wish to strengthen your speaking and even your conversational skills. There are several other benefits of active listening. In this chapter, I will show you why it is important to develop active listening skills. You are also going to learn the barriers that stand in the way of active listening, ways to listen more effectively, and how to encourage your audience to listen to your message. But before I dig into that, it is necessary to understand the difference between listening and hearing.

Hearing Is Not Listening

Saying "I can hear you" is very different from, "I am listening to you." Hearing is not listening. The truth is that if you don't have auditory disabilities, then hearing comes to you as a natural ability. You hear without any effort. Hearing is simply a response, as part of your physiological makeup, to sound waves that are traveling through the air. Sound waves are transmitted to the ears and into the brain where they are processed and interpreted for meaning. The sound undergoes auditory association in the brain where it is matched with previously encountered sounds. No physical effort is required for this process to occur as the mind of the hearer may be occupied with other thoughts or engaged in other tasks. Hearing is a passive human attribute; it occurs even while you are asleep.

Listening, on the other hand, goes far beyond the natural ability to receive and interpret sound. It goes further beyond hearing; it requires the person who receives the soundwaves to pay close attention to make sense and meaning of the sound. For example, a speaker that has been talking for a while can say to the audience, "please listen to this." She does this when she believes she has something to say that is important for the audience to note. Why would a speaker do this? There are chances that a good number of the audience members may not be listening at that moment, even when they seem to be staring at the speaker. To listen, greater attention needs to be paid; the listener must seek to grasp the message of the speaker.

Listening is an intentional act, contrary to hearing. It is also important to note that humans listen for different reasons.

There are five different types of listening. For example, when you listen to a song or an actor on television, it is more of a pleasure listening, known as appreciative listening. Lawyers, therapists, or counselors engage in empathetic or therapeutic listening. Relational listening involves actively listening to friends or family with the primary goal of strengthening the bond in a relationship. In a debate, as you listen to key points to better your understanding of an issue or a topic which in turn influences your judgment and enables you to organize a response, you engage your critical listening skills. Finally, when you are in an environment to learn, as in a seminar room or a church, you engage in informational listening.

As a speaker, it is not only important that you understand the difference between hearing and listening, it is also essential that you know the different kinds of listening and the best practices to engage your senses in improving your overall listening skills.

Why Is This Important?
If you are still wondering about the connection between active listening skills and your ability to speak effectively off-the-cuff, then imagine this scenario. You are in a meeting, hearing all that is said but not listening to the issues. Then suddenly, a

question is thrown at you, "So when do you think is the best time to implement this strategy and what would be your reasons?" There you are, not even sure of what strategy they are referring to, let alone suggest an appropriate time for implementation. Your ability to respond logically in this situation depends primarily on how closely you have been listening to the matters arising.

I cannot emphasize enough how important it is to improve your listening skills. The central benefit listening is knowledge-gathering, making a better sense of the world that you live in. Only if you just take your mind back, you will realize how much you've learned over the years just by listening.

Think about the academic benefits for a moment. There is a strong connection between academic success and active listening. The closer attention a student pays in class, the higher his/her performance.

Think about the professional benefits. Active listening helps you think critically and make better judgments and decisions. Sound listening skills is a strong attribute for effective leadership.

Think of the personal benefits. Did you learn from your parents as a kid? I suppose so. Did these lessons add any value to your life? If you are like me, then it did add value to your life. Did your parents write the lessons they wanted you to learn on paper? Absolutely not! At least I can say that about my parents. If you learned from them at all, it means that at some point, you listened. Although children learn from parents in many ways, listening is primary. What about your spiritual leader? Do you have one? Maybe a pastor, a priest, or an Imam, to mention a few. How do you learn from them? You listen. If only you can think for a moment, you would realize the power, the importance, and the benefits of active listening.

I can hear you say, "Oh…wait a minute! I thought this is a book about impromptu speaking." You are right, it is a book about impromptu speaking, and there is a strong connection between active listening and impromptu speaking.

As far as impromptu speaking is concerned, it is important

to discuss listening for three basic reasons:

Firstly, when you speak, you draw from the reservoir of your knowledge, and your knowledge is significantly enriched by how much and how well you listen.

Secondly, when you are asked a question, or when you are told to share your opinion based on a conversation, your response is effective when it is tied around the subject at hand. This is only possible when you are mentally engaged with the conversation, which fundamentally requires good listening.

Thirdly, your audience's attention is enhanced by your delivery, which can be strengthened by the adjustments you make as you get feedback (both verbal and nonverbal) from the audience.

Just like I mentioned in a previous chapter, speaking logically in impromptu situations has a lot to do with how much you know and how deep your understanding of an issue is. And these have much to do with how well you listen. The good news is that you can further expand the depth of your knowledge by improving upon your listening skills, as you will learn in this chapter.

Obstacles to Effective Listening

Can you name some obstacles to success? You should have a long list of them on your mind. In my mind, I can think of procrastination, laziness, indecision, inconsistency impatience, lack of focus, and the list goes on. It is the desire of everyone to succeed, but these barriers just get in the way, maybe because it is in human nature to follow the path of least resistance. But just as there are obstacles to success, there are also obstacles to active listening. While you try to listen, these obstacles stand in your way to frustrate your effort. Let us first address these obstacles before we look at ways to improve our listening skills.

When You Are Judgmental

Sometimes humans are quick to jump to conclusions and judge speakers. An ineffective listener might notice that a speaker mispronounces a word and then start to question the speaker's integrity, which may ultimately affect the way the listener receives the message. This should not be the case. Some people also get distracted by trivialities like the speaker's outfit, unfamiliar accent, bad hairstyle, voice texture, and other physical attributes. This attitude will weaken your ability to grasp a speaker's message. To become an active listener, you must disregard these minor errors and focus your attention on what the speaker has to say. Although it can sometimes be challenging to get your mind off some of these distractions, however, you must train yourself to do so.

Anticipation

Anticipating what the speaker will say is another obstacle to active listening. You might be listening to a speaker and, at the same time, making assumptions on what the speaker's next point would be. Or you could be thinking about how the speaker is going to conclude the speech. This is common among people who believe they know more than the speaker. It could be the case, but you can never tell what you can learn, even from a mediocre. According to Plutarch, "Know how to listen, and you will profit even from those who talk badly."

Assumed Comprehension

Sometimes listeners tend to assume they understand what the speaker is saying even when they lack genuine understanding. This is self-deception. As a listener, if you are in a situation where you can seek clarification from the speaker, be sure to do so to get a clearer understanding of the message. You could use phrases like: "Do you mean…", "Are you trying to say…", "What do you mean by…", and so on, to get clarification on issues.

Emotional Reactions

Paul, a participant in one of my classes, shared his experience with the class. He was a member of an audience in a seminar on leadership. While the speaker was talking, he mentioned the name of a leader in the financial (banking) sector in his country, but unfortunately, the leader had died. On hearing the name of the late banking chief, Paul was lost in his thoughts. He said for over five minutes, he wasn't listening to what the speaker was saying. He was thinking of how he loved the late bank chief executive and what a significant loss his exit was to the financial sector, and so on. This is an obstacle to listening. Such an emotional response to a speaker's statement will disrupt your listening. It can also happen when a speaker says something contrary to your beliefs, and you engage in a mental battle with them, causing you to stop listening altogether. Once your emotions crawl into the picture, active listening crawls out. Also, while it is ok to express empathy, don't let it stand as an obstacle.

Ways to Enhance Listening
Active listening is an essential skill to have in your communications belt. There is no doubt about that, and at least I have been able to establish this fact. But only the knowledge of how important it is to listen will not do you much good if you do not learn how to improve upon this critical communication skill. Take note of the following points to improve your listening skills.

Make up your mind to listen
To get the best out of what a speaker is saying, you must first decide to listen. When you make this decision, it affects your mindset and your attitude and disposition towards the speaker. It helps you focus on the speaker and the message. Your mind is present when you decide to listen. On the contrary, when you are not sure whether to listen or not, it becomes very easy for your mind to wander off to different thoughts.

Keep an open mind
You listen, not to hear what you want to hear, but to get an understanding of what the speaker has to say. You must keep an open mind while listening. Keeping an open mind helps prevent anticipations and assumptions, as mentioned earlier. It frees your mind from being on the defensive; however, it

opens your mind to understanding.

Control distractions

Distractions, if not checked, tend to setback your ability to listen effectively. These distractions often present themselves in environments where you are expected to listen. Some of these distractions are within your control. For example, the notifications from the increasing number of social networks, emails, text messages, and calls from your phone could be a distraction. Digital devices, especially mobile phones, are now an extension of ourselves. As difficult as it may be to disconnect yourself from your mobile phone, it is important to keep it out of sight when you intend to listen actively. It is within your control to do this.

On the other hand, there are other kinds of distractions that you cannot control. For example, a long time ago, I had a meeting with a group of people in an open space, a location that was our best option at that time. As we were discussing, I could hear from a distance a rendition of Bob Marley hit song "One Love." It was one of my favorite songs at a time. The song was a big distraction for me because I was singing along, not to the hearing of anyone present, but in my mind. It was a challenge. I was about halfway into the song when I reminded myself that I could always go home and play the song, as much as I wanted, but as for the meeting, I couldn't have a repeat of the exact proceedings.

Distractions are common. You must be able to identify them and keep your mind protected when you want to listen actively.

Take notes

Taking notes might not be possible in every setting, but when the environment is right to take notes, it is often helpful to do so while listening; as such, you are able to engage with what the speaker is saying. You must remember that your aim is not to take down the entire words of the speaker.

Your note-taking should focus on writing down important ideas, main points, and possible questions to ask the speaker when it is appropriate to do so.

Providing Feedback as a Listener

This area addresses listening from a speaker's perspective. It is essential to listen while you speak. As a speaker, you should be attentive to the ongoing feedback from your audience. The feedback from a listener is an important part of the communication process. The feedback that a listener offers to a speaker can affect the content and delivery of the speaker. When you speak, make sure you listen to feedback from your audience, both verbal and nonverbal feedback. So, when you take on the role of an audience member, be a good listener and provide positive feedback to the speaker. Let me share with you how you can give verbal and nonverbal feedback as a listener.

Nonverbal Feedback

Just imagine that you are speaking to an audience, and they are slumped in their chairs with their eyes closed and legs crossed. How would that make you feel as a speaker? The state of the audience will most likely affect your delivery and possibly, your confidence. This is because they are offering nonverbal feedback that simply says that your message is uninteresting and unimportant to them. Nicholas Boothman, in his book, "How to make people like you in 90 seconds or less," recommends listening with your whole body. This is very true about nonverbal forms of feedback.

Your head is a good place to start. Nodding constructively and affirmatively provides positive feedback to a speaker. Eye contact is another crucial nonverbal cue, indicating to the speaker that you are listening. Eye contact also helps you to concentrate. When your eyes wander, they take in images that are sent to your brain, which in turn affects your attention to the speaker.

Leaning-in, as a listener, is also a form of nonverbal feedback to the speaker. Calvin Miller, in his book "The Empowered Communicator," refers to this as the "Listener's Lean." He explains that leaning-in shows the listener's genuine interest and provides positive, reflexive, nonverbal feedback that endorses the communication.

Verbal Feedback

Echoing "Yes," "Uhum," "OK," etc. in response to a speaker are all verbal feedback that are very effective in helping the speaker measure your interest. But beyond this form of feedback is the art of questioning. Questioning is an effective way of offering verbal feedback to a speaker. As a listener, you demonstrate that you are paying attention by asking relevant questions that are related to what the speaker is saying. This is not just an arbitrary process merely directed at making the speaker feel good; it enhances your listening and helps you get a deeper understanding of what is said. By asking relevant questions, you also show that you have an interest in what the speaker is saying.

Questioning could take several forms. It could be direct open-ended questions to help the speaker elaborate more on the subject. It could also be in a manner that reflects the speaker's message; this involves repeating or paraphrasing what the speaker has said. It reinforces the speaker's message and also demonstrates your understanding. Questioning for clarification involves asking questions to ensure that you are receiving the correct message; this also enables the speaker to expand on specific points.

Move Beyond Hearing; Listen

Hearing is an arbitrary act; however, listening is an active and deliberate act. Active listening skills are essential to have as a speaker. Listening could be a difficult task, but it is worth every ounce of your effort. It is an important skill, and you must make a conscious effort to develop it.

When you are a good listener, you open an enormous opportunity to learn and grow, which is invaluable for you as a speaker.

CHAPTER EIGHT

Deliver With Impact

It is delivery that makes the orator's success.
-Johann Wolfgang

One afternoon, many years ago, I walked into a restaurant to get some food. I was very hungry. I made an order for a local dish; mashed yam and egusi soup. This was my favorite meal. After waiting for about five minutes, the waitress walked down to my table with my order. It was just exactly what I ordered and the same size as I expected it to be. But there was a problem. Not only was the food served with a very old dish, but I also noticed that the dish was not clean. Just at the edge of the round plate, there was dirt of some sort. Perhaps a dried food particle, probably from a previous order. It was obvious that the plate was not properly cleaned. As soon as I saw the poor state upon which the food was presented, I lost my appetite. I had to reject the food.

I rejected the food not because I was no longer hungry; I was still hungry. I needed the food, but I rejected it. Why? I rejected the food even though it was exactly what I ordered, simply because of how it was served. This is a perfect analogy when it comes to speeches, both long and short. Good content delivered poorly will not be received well by an audience. When your delivery is poor, your audience will reject your wisdom.

Delivery for Impromptu Speeches

Delivery is a crucial element of speaking. As much as what you say is important, how you say what you say is equally as important.

An impromptu speech, delivered poorly, will lose its power. Irrespective of the platform, a good delivery is of critical importance for an effective and impactful impromptu speech.

Regrettably, poor delivery can make even a speech with great content sound uninteresting or even meaningless. Conversely, good delivery can make even a speech with weak content seem compelling. Sometimes if you are not careful enough to pay close attention to what is said by a speaker with an excellent delivery skill, you could pass an empty and weak speech for a great one.

To prevent your impromptu speech from sounding monotonous, you must infuse life into every aspect of your delivery to captivate your audience. When you do this, you inevitably make your speech impactful.

At its best, good delivery should make every audience member, regardless of size, feel as if they're in a personal conversation with you.

A Closer Look at Delivery

There are several components of delivery. In this chapter, I am going to break down the concept of delivery for an impromptu speech into two parts. Firstly, I will address what you should do before you start speaking, and secondly, I will explain what you need to do when you start speaking.

Before You Speak

It is not in all cases that you find yourself caught off-guard speaking impromptu. Sometimes, you are aware that you will be responding to questions or speaking impromptu in other capacities. In these moments, you must embrace the right frame of mind so that you can give your best. These are the following things that you must consider.

Consider Your Audience

You must not forget that the reason why you are speaking in the first place is because you have an audience; there is somebody to listen to whatever you have to say. Apart from your audience, your speech would just be a private conversation with yourself, which does not apply to our current subject. What I need you to understand is that your audience is the most important aspect in any kind of public speaking setting.

But the question here is, how does your audience impact your delivery? Think of a professor responding to the question of a student in the presence of students as against the same professor's response in the presence of other professors. Do you think the difference in audience class would impact the delivery? Most definitely! You would expect that the professor will be more deliberate, emphatic, and careful among fellow professionals, especially if they are more experienced. On the contrary, the same professor will be more carefree with the students.

Another example would be an employee speaking before the CEO and other directors as against speaking before colleagues of the same level. You could also imagine a preacher teaching a congregation as against the same preacher's message to fellow preachers. The list goes on.

What I need you to understand is the importance of considering your relationship with your audience when thinking about delivery. Align your delivery in such a way that it is most effective for your audience at every given time. When you do this, your audience will always be positively disposed to your message. This is true for both impromptu speeches and other formal and lengthier speeches.

Consider Yourself

Responding logically requires that you put your mind and body in a proper condition. The state of your mind and body is essential when it comes to delivery. There are several things to have in mind when considering yourself.

Firstly, you must be confident. I discussed this in chapter two. No matter how unprepared you are, never give in to fear, especially when you are called upon to speak or respond to a question that seems difficult to answer. Fear is always counterproductive to your effectiveness in any form of speaking. When you entertain fear, it disorganizes your thoughts, quickly saps every element of confidence that you have remaining within you, and leaves you empty and stranded.

If impromptu speaking is what you do regularly, this shouldn't be a challenge. You should have the confidence to handle the situation. But if this is not the case, then there are just a few things you can do to overcome every form of fear at the spur of the moment. Like I mentioned earlier, you must take advantage of deep breathing at this point. Breathing deeply does a lot more for you than you can imagine. When you do this, you ease every form of tension; you get more oxygen to circulate in your bloodstream, especially towards your brain; with this, you are more relaxed and well able to access your knowledge base.

Secondly, while you feel confident within, you must allow this confidence to reflect without. When you are required to walk to a podium; Rise slowly. Don't slump, if you are standing, stand tall. Don't fidget or put your hands in your pockets. Always ensure to display confidence.

For occasions where you are sure that you would be speaking impromptu, as the case of an interview, your appearance is important. Dress in a way that presents you as someone that is intelligible and credible. Your appearance can also boost your confidence.

Consider the Platform

There are several platforms where you might be asked to speak impromptu. You might be asked to speak impromptu in various settings: during interviews, deliberative meetings like board meetings, occasions that call for impromptu remarks, on a cable network, or even in debates. The specific platform on which you speak can influence your style of delivery. For example, your gestures and movements are limited when speaking impromptu over the air. On air, your voice is your strongest instrument of delivery.

You must consider the platform upon which you are about

to speak and marshal every delivery component that would make your speech impactful and memorable on such a platform.

When You Speak

When you start speaking, ensure your speech is delivered effectively to achieve the desired impact. As far as speech delivery is concerned, there are two areas that you must take note of. The first is the vocal components of delivery, and the second is the physical components of delivery. The vocal components of delivery include those elements of speaking that relate to your voice, while the physical components of delivery include those elements of delivery that concern your body. Both components must come together, in most cases, for your delivery to be effective. Let's look into these components of delivery to get a better understanding of how you can make them work well in your speeches.

Vocal Components of Delivery

When you speak, your voice is the primary medium through which your spoken message travels and eventually reaches your audience. There are several elements to the human voice that you hear. What you must do is pay very close attention to these elements as you speak. Take note of the following aspect of the voice as you speak.

Pronunciation

Your ability to accurately pronounce words is an asset and a big plus during verbal communication. Correct pronunciation helps your audience get a clearer meaning of the message you intend to pass across. This is important because your ability to pronounce words accurately enhances your credibility as a speaker. Wrong pronunciations tend to distract listeners.

Articulation

Articulation is also a very important aspect of delivery. What this means is that you treat every word that you utter with special attention. It means starting and completing every word you say. This is also a very powerful credibility booster for speakers. Clear articulation and mumbling exist on a spectrum of speech clarity. Generally, as one's articulation diminishes, the tendency to mumble can increase.

Pitch

This is the highness or lowness of a speaker's voice. Naturally, the human pitch tends to change, going up and down even when we don't pay attention to it, particularly during regular conversations. This variation of pitch, which is referred to as inflection, gives effect to the words that you say; it communicates meaning and emotion. Paying closer attention to it and enhancing its effects during impromptu speeches serves well as an effective delivery component.

Unfortunately, what happens most of the time with amateur during an impromptu speech or any other form of public speaking is that their pitch becomes monotonous. A monotonous delivery tends to sap out the "humanness" in your voice, making you sound more like a machine or a robot. When you notice that you sound monotonous, it's ok to pause, take a quick deep breath, and make the necessary adjustment.

Volume

This is the loudness or softness of a speaker's voice. One of your goals, when you speak, should be to be heard by everyone listening. This is because no matter how good your speech is, it would be useless if it is not heard by your audience. So, when you are speaking, ensure to control the volume of your voice in a manner that you are heard by everyone in the audience. Volume control is very important as a speaker. You must be able to control the volume of your voice while speaking.

Tone

I would describe tone as the manner of speaking that is often an indicator of the speaker's thought or feeling. The tone is very important when speaking, as it helps convey your emotions and interests. If you speak with a low variance in your tone, or monotonously, your audience will easily lose interest in what you are saying. Such a tone creates the impression that you are not even interested in what you are saying. You must vary your tone and always keep it lively.

Rate

This is the pace at which you speak. Some people are naturally fast speakers, while some other people speak at a slower pace. This is also a very core aspect of delivery. Rate could be a distinguishing factor between ideas of high and low importance. For example, when you race over an important point, the impact on the audience is reduced, and the message also stands a great chance of losing its meaning.

Your pace also affects the listener's perception of what you are saying. It is good as a speaker to emphasize important points when speaking. To do this, you will need to speak slowly.

Another very important reason for speaking slowly is that it gives you time to think as you speak. It is a great opportunity to structure your thought in the most logical and persuasive manner. I am not undermining the idea of speaking fast. The truth is that there are people who speak fast and still organize their thoughts nicely. However, when you reduce your pace, it gives your audience more time to process what you are saying.

Pause

Pause is a very powerful and highly effective delivery component. Pausing can drastically change how your message is received. It helps to punctuate your speech. It can also be used to highlight important points.

Pausing can also help you avoid the interference of verbal "viruses" (meaningless words & fillers) such as um, uh, ah, etc., that often infiltrate most impromptu speeches. These fillers present you as someone who is not very confident or sure of what he/she is saying; they could distract your audience. They dilute the impact of your message. However, with the help of strategic pauses, you can get rid of them.

In addition, strategic pauses not only give your audience a moment to think through what you have said, it also gives you time as the speaker to organize your thought. If you feel like you don't know what to say next, just take a pause. You will be surprised how much information will come to you when you pause.

Physical Components of Delivery

Just as you transmit your message to your audience through your voice, your body also sends signals to your audience while you speak. There are also several components to physical delivery, and these components perform several functions at several moments as you speak.

Facial Expression

Facial expressions are important throughout the duration of your speech. It communicates your feelings and emotions. Your facial expression should reflect the emotions associated with what you are saying. To show you how important facial expressions are, there are movies where the lead cast communicates to its viewers, just with facial expressions and gestures. The famous "Mr. Bean" series is a good example. Also, you must remember that the occasion should determine your facial expression. You don't want to keep a serious countenance when telling a joke. Be sure that your facial expressions mirror the tone of your speech and the occasion.

Eye Contact

This refers to how and how often a speaker looks at audience members during a speech. This is a very important aspect of delivery. A speaker must not glance vaguely at the audience. Your eye contact as you speak, must be deliberate as though you are having a conversation with somebody. This is a powerful way to connect with members of the audience.

Most people suggest that a speaker should keep eye contact

with one person in the audience or with someone at the back of the room. Doing this would limit the effect or relevance of eye contact as an effective delivery component. You must remember that the primary function of eye contact is to help you create a relationship with the audience. My suggestion is that you make eye contact with several members of your audience. You must also remember that this is only possible for an audience that is close enough for you to make eye contact.

Posture

Your posture refers to the position of your body when you speak. When standing, ensure that you stand up straight and have your feet in a relaxed and natural pose. Also, when sitting, sit up straight. This not only conveys confidence; it also helps the quality of your voice. Please remember, a slack posture makes you look dull and creates the impression that you are uncomfortable.

Gesture

Communication is not limited to the voice and eyes alone. The way you use your legs, hands, and body also communicate nonverbal messages to your audience. Most times, a gesture can convey to your audience a message that several words can't. Even when you are saying something meaningful, your gesture or the lack of it could be saying, "I am tired," "I am nervous," "I am energetic," to mention a few.

Also, you must remember that the use of gestures should be controlled in a manner that does not distract your audience. There is a valuable suggestion that hand gestures should be kept within the "gesture box." The gesture box is an imaginary square that extends from your shoulders, through your chest region and down to the lower abdomen. Most of your hand gestures should be kept within this box. This is not a fixed rule, but it can help you keep your gesture in check.

Brevity and Impromptu Speech

Brevity is very important when it comes down to the subject of delivery. This is important to note because most people fall into the temptation of wanting to go on and on, because they know too much about the subject. This is not the best for an impromptu speech. Limit your points and go straight to them. You stand the risk of rambling when you dwell too much on your speech. Also, you could lose your audience if you keep talking nonstop. Your audience can only take so much. Remember this: "Keep It Succinct and Simple" (KISS). This should be your watchword. Don't underestimate the power of simplicity.

Deliver It Hot

You may have a great idea to share, and you may be able to present it logically, but if you don't deliver it effectively, it will lose its desired impact. This is not what you want. Delivery is a relevant component in the art of speaking, both in impromptu and other lengthier speeches. Different delivery styles can alter the way a speech is received by an audience. Every appropriate aspect of delivery should be used effectively if you want your message to be impactful. Your impromptu speeches must be delivered hot.

CHAPTER NINE

Becoming a Critic

Criticism, like rain, should be gentle enough to nourish a man's growth without destroying his roots.
-Frank A. Clark

In your journey to excellence in impromptu speaking, you must develop a heart for criticism. That is, you must become an impromptu speech critic. But before you begin, you must ask yourself questions about this subject of criticism. Why is it necessary to critique impromptu speeches? Why must you critique other people when they speak impromptu? How does it affect your ability to speak effectively in impromptu situations?

From previous chapters, I have been able to establish that a successful impromptu speech should be coherent, logical, and persuasive, with well-organized content, and should be delivered with grace and charisma. The more effectively you can identify an impromptu speech that is well delivered, the more skillful you would be in identifying what you are doing wrong in your own impromptu speeches and the greater your chances for improvement. Studying, evaluating, and critiquing the effectiveness and techniques of other speakers is, beyond doubt, an excellent way to become better at giving impromptu speeches. But your attempt to learn from these criticisms must be deliberate.

Studying the techniques used by brilliant speakers in impromptu speeches gives you an abundant supply of ideas that could be easily incorporated into your style or technique. You will be armed with a broad knowledge of styles and techniques. You will be able to identify what works and what doesn't work. When a speaker lacks impact, you can quickly discern their shortcomings and suggest improvements. But remember, as you critique others, it is even more important to critique yourself.

You Must Also Check Yourself

It is not just enough for you to study the speeches of other people. While you work on your performance in delivering impromptu speeches, you must conduct self-evaluations and critique your own speeches. As you gain a deeper understanding of how impromptu speaking works, you must continuously check for areas where you need to improve. You must go beyond the cognitive process of understanding and effectively interpreting the ills of a weak speech to having a strong practical knowledge of what is happening in your own performances.

As I mentioned in the chapter on practice, video and audio recordings are great resources for evaluating yourself. They capture your performance in real life and give you the opportunity to go over your delivery as many times as you wish, helping you identify your areas of strength and the areas where you need improvement. Having other people evaluate your speech is also very useful in monitoring your performance. Again, joining a Toastmasters club could be very helpful in this regard.

Evaluate the Speech

The ability to study and evaluate other speakers is a critical skill. This ability will no doubt accelerate your growth as a speaker. There are several elements that go into the mix of an excellently delivered impromptu speech. To critique a speech, it is necessary for you to closely examine and evaluate these elements individually. On a basic level, these elements include the structure of the speech, the content, and the delivery components.

The Content and Structure
The content of the impromptu speech is basically what is most important to the audience. This is what they will take home. Your goal as a speaker is to convey the content of your speech in a manner that will be impactful. To make the content of the speech have the desired impact, it must fit into the structure that is required for such speech, as discussed in an earlier chapter. The content should be spread into an introduction, a body, and a conclusion. Every aspect of the speech should be evaluated.

The Introduction
The impromptu speech is short, and so the introduction is not elaborate. It could be a single sentence or several sentences but not as lengthy as a prepared speech. You must evaluate the success of an introduction by asking the following questions.

Did the speaker use any form of attention getter to draw the audience into the other parts of the speech? This could be a statistic, a joke, a shocking statement, a question, a quote? Was the attention-getter effective? Was it in place? Was it relevant for the speech? For example, the speaker could tell a joke that has been overused, which in turn might not evoke laughter from the audience. If there is an attention-getter, it must be effective.

Was the opening memorable? When asked about his take on sex trade, Adam, a human rights activist, made a memorable opening statement. He said, "Before the end of this discourse in about an hour time, at least one hundred young innocent girls will be sold for sex trafficking." That is a visual, effective, and memorable opening statement for an impromptu speech. Can such an opening statement make you think again about human rights violations? It should.

The Body
This is the main part of the speech, where the speaker states his points or make or support an argument. To critique this part of the speech, you must ask the following questions:

Was the speech focused? A speech that has several unrelated points that are not addressing the objective of the speech is not focused. If you are asked to talk briefly on the dangers of drug abuse among teenagers, it would be unnecessary to start explaining how drugs are transported into the country. A speaker must be focused.

Was the speech organized, was it laid out in a logical manner? There are some speeches that lack organizational flow. What you want is to have every element of the speech working together to support a common objective. The arguments, stories, data, etc. must all relate to the primary objective of the speech.

How effectively did the speaker transition throughout the speech? Were you able to identify the different parts of the speech with the help of the speaker's transitions? Transitional words and phrases, as mentioned, are very useful tools for speakers. A good use of them in a speech will help the audience follow through the different parts of the speech.

That a speech is delivered impromptu does not mean it should lack useful information. The speech must be educational. Did you feel like you learned anything from the speaker? Was the speech informative?

The Conclusion

Just like the introduction in the impromptu speech, the conclusion can be a single statement or maybe several statements. These statements should be concise and should restate the objective of the speech. Did the speaker consider this in the conclusion? Also, depending on the objective of the speech, was there a call to action? These are core elements of a conclusion that you must look out for when critiquing a speech.

Important Delivery Components

Poor content delivered well can have a stronger impact on the audience than good content that is poorly delivered. It is just like having an inexperienced or wannabe pianist playing a beautiful grand piano. You are most certainly going to hate the sound that is produced and would even regard it as noise. This would annoy you even more if you just heard a maestro play that same piano. Although it is the same piano, the output is different. Critiquing a speaker's delivery is very important.

Giving feedback on a speaker's delivery is an area that is crucial and beneficial for a speaker, since evaluating one's own body language and style can be challenging. It is therefore important to give the speaker a gentle but honest critique of the effectiveness of his or her delivery. The efficiency in executing your feedback comes from isolating each component of delivery, addressing them separately, and posing key questions.

Gestures
Where it is applicable, look closely at the speaker's posture and body language. Does it display a high level of poise, charisma, and confidence? Was the speaker's gesture spontaneous and uncontrolled, or was it natural, timely, and purposeful? Were the gestures meaningful? Were there any overtly repetitive gestures or other mannerisms that were distracting to the audience? These are important questions to ask when evaluating a speaker's gesture.

Vocal Variety
Nobody enjoys listening to a monotonous speaker; however, a speaker that uses vocal variety gives life to a speech and makes the speech easy to listen to. Was the speaker easy to hear? Listen to the speaker's voice inflections. Did the speaker apply loud and soft variations to the voice?

Rate/Pause
Some speakers talk too fast so that it becomes difficult to follow along with them. The speaker must not be too fast to the extent that it becomes difficult to follow along and also not too slow that the speech begins to sound boring. The speaker's pace should favor the comprehension of the listeners. See if

the person is speaking at a pace that sounds natural and easy to understand. Were pauses used in the speech? Were the pauses used in a manner that highlighted important points to increase the impact of the points? Pauses are useful tools in delivery and must be used appropriately and effectively. A great speaker knows when to pause for the desired effect.

Eye Contact

Where applicable, did the speaker use eye contact effectively to connect with the audience? Was the speaker's gaze fixed on just a segment of the audience? The role of the eyes in speaking is not arbitrary; it must be deliberately used to enhance connection with the audience no matter the size?

Pronunciation/Articulation

Did you hear clearly the words of the speaker? Where there mispronunciations? This is important to note because when there are mispronunciations and when the speaker's words are poorly articulated, it could distract the audience and even weaken the effect of the message.

Language

Did the speaker use a language that is appropriate for the audience? What are the stylistic devices used? Where they used effectively and appropriately? (Although you can't judge the effectiveness of a speaker by the absence of style) Did you notice any technical jargon or unnecessary use of slang? Listen for verbal pauses or filler words like "Um," "Uh," "Ah," etc." Using filler words scarcely can be pardonable; they should not overwhelm the speech. Using it excessively in a speech steals from a speaker's credibility. Having zero filler words in your speech should be the aim of a speaker.

Giving a Constructive Feedback

As previously mentioned, critiquing impromptu speeches plays a vital role in your process of becoming a skilled impromptu speaker. While you could critique these speeches as much as you like without any obligation, you may also find yourself in an environment where you are required to critique a speech and immediately give a constructive feedback to the speaker.

An example is the case of a Toastmasters Club, where you can be assigned to give feedback to a speaker. In this situation, you must be prepared. Have a notebook and a pen ready to take detailed notes during the speech, organizing your notes to address both the content and delivery components of the speech. On the other hand, you could also request for feedback on your speech from someone who is competent in the art of speaking impromptu or someone good at evaluating speeches.

Remember, the goal for giving constructive feedback is to improve the abilities and competencies of a speaker and, similarly, receiving constructive feedback improves your competence with impromptu speeches. When you understand how crucial the ability to critique effectively is, you will be more dedicated to becoming competent at it. To guide you through how to give effective feedback, consider the following points.

Address the Issues and Not the Person
Have you ever received feedback that made you feel bad? It's likely you've received such feedback before. What happens afterward is that you spend most of your time trying to attend to your wounded emotion instead of having a clearer understanding of what went wrong and how to improve your skills. This kind of feedback directs harsh comments at the speaker's personality instead of the area for growth. This is not a proper way to give feedback. When you give feedback in this manner, it tends to deflate the interest rather than improve the understanding of the individual under evaluation. The proper approach to giving feedback is to separate the individual from the issues and address those issues.

For example, it would be wrong to tell a speaker, "It seems like you are not good at telling jokes. Just find other ways to open your speech." This is a direct attack at the speaker, which is not only inappropriate but also unprofessional. Revising the feedback, you could say, "Your joke was funny, but it didn't work well with the main idea of the speech." Putting it this way addresses the issue and not the person, and most importantly, it throws light on the area that needs improvement.

Be Specific

"I think you need to improve your delivery." "Your speech was not coherent enough." "I found it very difficult to follow along with your speech." These statements, when they stand alone, are too vague to serve as practical and useful feedback. Unfortunately, I have seen many people give feedback in this manner, not breaking down the issues into specific details, which are essential in making feedback actionable. An effective feedback must address specific areas of a speech, as observed by the evaluator.

If you are still wondering what could be wrong with the above statements as feedbacks, then take the first one on delivery for example. The term delivery is broad as far as giving a speech is concerned. There are several components under the concept of speech delivery, like posture, eye contact, vocal delivery, just to mention a few. Therefore, telling a speaker, "I think you need to improve on your delivery," is neither specific nor actionable. A better way to say this could be, "You need to do a little more work in engaging your audience with effective eye contact and also increasing the volume of your voice," and so on. This way, the speaker has a clearer understanding of what needs to be worked on.

What about the feedback regarding coherence and the difficulty of following the speech? There are different aspects of a speech that could make this happen. For example, a speech will not be coherent if, for instance, a support that is supposed to be for point (A) is misplaced and mentioned after point (B). And a speech would be difficult to follow if all the points and segments of the speech are muddled together without proper transitions within the speech. As an evaluator, you must let the speaker know the specifics.

The Feedback Sandwich Method

When you give feedback, it is equally important to point out what was done right as it is to mention areas that need improvement. If you're working with someone who needs help improving their speaking skills, be as encouraging as possible so that they are encouraged to keep working and improving on their speaking skills. You can achieve this by using the feedback sandwich method.

The feedback sandwich method starts with a compliment on what the speaker did well, followed by an area that needs improvement, then another compliment, and so on. This means sandwiching negative feedback between two positive comments, or a weakness between two strengths.

For example, you could start your feedback by telling the person how good the introduction was, but that the first point was not convincing because there was no form of support to it. However, the second point was strong and did support the main idea of the speech. Starting with a positive comment or compliment helps the speaker feel comfortable, allowing them to understand that you are on their side and not merely criticizing them. Then after the negatives or criticism, ensure to end with a compliment. When you do this, you leave the speaker motivated as against ending with a negative, an approach that leaves a speaker with bad feelings. This method of delivering constructive criticism makes the feedback easy to receive.

Give Useful Recommendations for Improvement

Feedback is given so that a speaker can make adjustments and ultimately improve. This is particularly true when the recommendations are useful.

Recommendations help to put criticisms in the right perspective, letting the receiver see exactly what you have in mind. This is because the receiver might have a different interpretation of the message that they receive. Giving recommendations, improves understanding.

For a recommendation to be effective it must be specific,

tailored to address a particular problem, and a reason must be stated to support the recommendation. Consider the examples below.

Poor recommendation: "This is too long to be an impromptu speech. Try and keep your impromptu speeches short. You could revise the points, make your introduction shorter or even limit your supports..."

This is not a very effective recommendation. It is not specific enough and might limit the receiver's ability to act on it. In contrast, a better recommendation would be:

Good recommendation: "Your introductory story was quite lengthy; summarizing it would give it more impact and keep it closer to your main point. Similarly, you used too many examples to support your points. Keeping it down to one or two supporting examples would make the speech more compact as too many examples may distract your listeners. Doing these would help you deliver a shorter 2-5 minutes speech with greater impact."

This is a better way to give a recommendation. It tells the speaker exactly what needs to be done.

There Is Strength in Criticism
The word criticism may sound harsh and maybe received negatively, but when you criticize an impromptu speech, you are not being negative; you are only strengthening your competence in the art. And the more you do this, the deeper insight you gain, and the better you understand what this is all about. Your ability to effectively criticize an impromptu speech is, therefore, of utmost importance and must not be neglected but worked on. When you do this, you will notice how it affects your competence over time.

CHAPTER TEN

Practicing for Success

Take advantage of every opportunity to practice your communication skills so that when important occasions arise, you will have the gift, the style, the sharpness, the clarity, and the emotions to affect other people.
-Jim Rohn

So far, in the preceding chapters of this book, I have mentioned several things that you could do to increase your understanding of impromptu speeches and some methods that would help you in delivering these speeches effectively and logically. I will provide more tips in this chapter. However, there is one thing you need to know about speaking well in an impromptu situation. No matter how many times you read this book, it will be almost useless if you don't put the highlighted concepts into practice. You should never underestimate the role of practice in mastering impromptu speaking. As Gandhi rightly said, "An ounce of practice is worth more than a ton of preaching." Attaining excellence in any profession or endeavor requires practice. Giving effective impromptu speeches is not an exception; you must practice if you want to master the art.

Impromptu Is Not Always Impromptu

One night, I was at my parents' house for a brief visit. I was watching a political show on TV with my mother. On the show, the host interview public figures around the country. On this episode, I guess the host had personal resentment for his guest, or maybe he had too much caffeine. He was relentless and brutal with his questioning, barraging the guest with questions from different angles. It felt like he was trying to carve a path to the guest's soul. But that was not the only amazing thing; the guest was badass.

Just as the question drops, he picks it up and does justice to it, answering every question most profoundly and articulately. They both went back and forth at an amazing pace and rhythm. It was almost like a fighting match.

My mom was dazed as the guest answered every single question almost without thinking. My mom was impressed. "He is very intelligent," she said, "these are difficult questions."

"That's right," I said. "But do you know how many times he had been asked these questions?"

"Whatever the case," my mom said with a smile on her face, "I just like the way he talks."

"There is no doubt about that," I said reassuringly, "I like the way he talks too" "but you must understand that this man has been a politician for a long time, so it is not a surprise that he is this witty."

I am sure you can think of several occasions when you were impressed at the way someone spoke off-the-cuff, maybe on TV or somewhere else. The truth is that impromptu is not always impromptu. Even, there are cases where the interview questions are sent to the guest before the show, although this is not the object of this chapter.

In this chapter, we shall be looking at the concept of practice from different perspectives; how to practice, how not to practice, different ways to practice, and resources for practicing effectively for impromptu speeches.

The Truth About Practice
When it comes down to the art of speaking effectively in impromptu situations, you must put in enough practice beyond the point of mastery; this is how you reach peak performance. This shouldn't scare you; it is an important skill, and it is worth the effort.

Alaa Ahmed, an assistant professor at the University of Colorado with two of her colleagues, published a research in the Journal of Neuroscience. In their study, they asked participants to move a cursor on a screen by manipulating a robotic arm. As they did so, the researchers measured the participants' energy expenditure by analyzing how much oxygen they inhaled and how much carbon dioxide they exhaled.

When the participants first attempted the exercise, they used up a lot of metabolic power, but this decreased as their skill improved. By the end of the learning process, the amount of effort they expended to carry out the task had declined about 20 Percent from when they started.

Over the course of a practice session, the subjects in the study were becoming more efficient in their muscle activity. Energy expenditures continued to decrease even after the decline in muscle activity had stabilized. Ahmed and her co-authors report that when it seems like nothing is happening as the participants carried out the task, is when the greatest reductions in metabolic power were observed.

They explain that even after participants had fine-tuned their muscle movements, the neural processes controlling the movements continued to grow more efficient. The brain uses up energy too, and through what they called "overlearning," it can get by on less.

Other research studies have demonstrated in one way or another that for a wide range of academic and professional activities, "overlearning" reduces the amount of mental effort and energy required to complete specific tasks, leading to a high performance.

The message from this study is that in order to perform with less effort, keep on practicing, even after it seems the task has been learned," says Ahmed. "We have shown there is an advantage to continued practice beyond any visible changes in performance." In other words: You're getting better and better, even when you can't tell you're improving."

Ephraim, a 22-year-old graduate, worked an interim job as a customer care representative at a telecommunication company.

His job role was to attend to customers' inquiries, requests, and complaints over the phone. When speaking with a customer, it is required that he input the customer's information and the details of their conversation into a computer application at the same time.

He reports that on the first day on the job and a few weeks following, he found it almost impossible to attend to both tasks at the same time. He would have to round up a call with a customer and, after that, input the necessary details into the application. But over time, as he mastered the art of communicating effectively with customers and operating the computer application efficiently, and, as the need to multitask increased, he was able to effortlessly run both tasks at the same time without thinking about it. This is what practice can do.

Why Practice for Impromptu Speeches?

When you think of impromptu speeches, you might be tempted to believe that it is not an art that can be practiced, probably because it is done at the spur of the moment. But fortunately, this is not the case. You can become very good at impromptu speaking by practicing.

I had an acquaintance by the name Joe who knew much about physical exercises and workouts. He could tell you several workout programs that you could do to develop any muscle group in the body. He knew the right diet that you would need to gain or lose weight as you exercise. He had a lot of books and magazines on this subject. One time he said to me, "Solonzo" the name he calls me, "It is not advisable to work on two different large muscle groups at the same time." He was the one that also advised me not to lift weight and do long roadwork on the same day. He was indeed an expert in the subject of exercising and workouts. But guess what? He was lazy as hell.

He was regular at the gym because he desired a nice physique. But all he did was talk. He was more of a spectator at the gym than an actor. He would talk and disturb others while they are busy working out. Because of this, his muscles were not as developed as he desired. He was fat.

I don't want you to be like Joe. You should put to practice everything that you learn here. It is vital to make it a point of duty to step up your game in this aspect of communication. Finding yourself in impromptu situations is unavoidable. As you make progress in life, the likelihood for such events continuously increases. You must make an effort to see that you increase your competence in this area.

Ways to Practice for Impromptu Speaking

To gain mastery and expertise in delivering effective impromptu speeches, you must practice. You must give enough time for practice to understand the methods that work and those that don't work. The more you practice, the more you develop a deeper understanding of the structural pattern of these speeches in real life. Practice also increases the nimbleness of your mind; that ability to quickly dig out information from your mental storehouse and organize them.

There are several available methods that have been developed to help with the practice of impromptu speeches, most of which require a quick and organized mental response to various subjects.

Impromptu Speeches Exercises

Exercise One

The first on this list is the speed thinking exercise. Its primary function is to aid the process of recalling information. To carry out this exercise, write down a major subject on a sheet of paper, like healthcare, music, books, economics, etc., and in sixty seconds list as many titles as you can, that falls under the subject.

To help you understand this exercise better, let's take the subject "War" for example. The possible words that come to mind when you think of war could be: Hunger, guns, death, displacement, pain, violence, hatred, explosion, fear, conflict, warfare, combat, fighting, soldiers, bloodshed, struggle, battle, skirmish, fight, clash, engagement, offensive, defense, attack, casualties, hostilities, weapons, scuffle, nations, aggression, destruction, mortality, military, civilians, genocide, rape, power, massacre, revolution, bomb, to mention a few.

This exercise is very useful for verbal fluency in impromptu speaking. It will help you think of words easily, especially those words that relate to a subject of discussion.

Exercise Two

I call this the Interview fabrication exercise. To carry out this exercise, you need to visit a news blog, listen on radio or watch any news channel on television, and as you get informed on any news, fabricate a question or a topic and immediately respond to it. For example, if you read about a rape case in the news, you could ask yourself, "What can the government do to reduce the cases of rape in the country?" After asking yourself this question, try to respond as quickly as possible. Apart from the news, you could also fabricate questions from other form of media.

While carrying out this exercise, ensure that your response to the questions flows in line with the structure, pattern, and strategies that have been outlined for delivering impromptu speeches. You could record your response so that you can go back and review it.

Note: It is important for you to always pay close attention to the news. Apart from the need to be updated and well informed, it is embarrassing when you are asked a question that is common news, and you can't answer, just because you have no idea of what they're talking about. So, you must stay informed and updated.

Exercise Three

In this third exercise, try to put together a long list of different topics on various subjects. And to practice, randomly select a topic from your list and discuss the topic. You could discuss each topic from different perspectives. This is a great resource for practicing impromptu speaking. You should go over your list until you are conversant with the topics. This exercise takes time, but it is worth the effort. Your list should be constantly updated. When putting topics together, center your thoughts around these areas; Current events, ideas, words, objects, quotations, proverbs, phrases, names, policies, etc. At the end of this book is a list of topics that you can practice with.

Exercise Four
I first experienced this exercise in a Toastmasters club. A member of the club was assigned to provide several topics. Each topic was written on a small rectangular sheet of white paper. All the topics were put together in a bowl, and each member of the club that was present came out, one after the other, picked a topic from the bowl, and delivered it impromptu. This is a very good way to practice impromptu speaking in a group. You could also do it on your own.

Exercise Five
This exercise involves the use of quotations for practice. Can you recite any quotation by heart? Think for a moment. Can you? Quotations are helpful in delivering brilliant impromptu speeches. They are helpful in two ways.

Firstly, quotations serve as excellent impromptu speech prompt. That means you can read a quotation and then discuss what you make of the quote. Take this quotation for example, "There can be no deep disappointment where there is not deep love" by Martin Luther King, Jr. What do you make of this quote?

The more reps you have reacting to quotations, the more insight you gain on how to structure your content and outline your thought logically.

Secondly, quotations can give you a quick start to some speech prompts. There are some topics that can easily be related to a quotation. If you have some of these quotes memorized, you can start of your speech by first reciting them and then linking the quotation to the subject matter. Using them effectively will help you begin your speech on a reasonably strong note.

Exercise Six

When driving or walking (if you are shy, then do this in a lonely road) or even when you are sitting in a park or any other public area, talk about the things you see as you drive, walk or sit. The fact is that you can make a speech from everything you see around you. You could talk about a building that was recently erected or about how the road has developed over the years or maybe the density of traffic on that road. The list of what you can talk about is endless.

Exercise Seven

I call this one the story mining exercise. It is one of the most important exercises that you can do, not just for impromptu speeches but other forms of oral communication. This has to do with mining stories from your personal life and experiences, as well as those of friends, family, and acquaintances. Turn these experiences into compelling stories. Remember, a story well narrated is memorable, persuasive, and more powerful than an excellent speech without a story.

Rehearse these stories and have them ready for use when the need arises.

I was going through personal story mining with a client in my private coaching at www.homeofinfluence.com. The client was amazed at the number of stories we were able to mine from her experiences. You may think you don't have a story to share until you start mining.

These are several methods that can be used to practice impromptu speaking. When you commit yourself to practice, you transform your speaking ability tremendously. You will be amazed at how good you can get by going through those exercises.

When practicing, always respond to the prompt vocally, don't be tempted to respond to them in your mind. Giving your response vocally gives you a clearer perspective of what you are saying, also by doing this, you can record your speeches for complete feedback and analysis.

Make it a point of duty to practice as often as possible, until you reach a good level of expertise. Practice! Practice! Practice! That is the name of the game. Practice with family, friends, strangers, and even animals, and you will be glad you did.

How Not to Practice

Have you ever taken the time to observe the practice sessions of most people? Or have you ever observed the way you practice? If you have, what do you notice? What do you think is common with the way most people practice, no matter what they are practicing? Most people engage in mere repetition, going over the presentation ten times or going over and over the speech until you feel it's good enough. This not to say that you don't get results eventually when you practice by repetition. You get results, but it is not a very effective way to practice, both for impromptu speeches and any other endeavor.

Why is mere repetition considered ineffective for practice? Firstly, it can delay the time it would take for you to attain excellence. This is because, by mere repetition, you deny your brain the task of achieving a specific result. Secondly, you stand the risk of giving up on the process because of how tedious and boring it could be to repeat a process continuously. This could hurt your confidence. But the contradiction here is that effective practice also involves repetition, in this case, a "mindful" repetition.

Practice Must Be Deliberate

Effective practice sessions must be deliberate. Deliberate practice is a systematic and highly structured process, unlike mindless repetition.

Deliberate practice involves monitoring your performance and continually looking for new ways to improve.

While practicing for impromptu speeches, it is advisable to

record your delivery on an audio or video recording device. Your phone will serve well in this regard. When you do this, you can easily listen to your delivery. As such, you can evaluate yourself and point out the areas of your speech that needs improvement. Evaluate your speech in terms of structure, content, strategy, and vocal delivery. Take the time to stop, analyze what went wrong, why it happened, and how you can improve. This is what a mindful and deliberate practice entails.

Practice for Success

Please remember, your goal is to speak effectively and logically when you speak impromptu. I want you to know that you can achieve this; you can speak intelligently every time in impromptu situations. But this will not happen by chance or even by providence. You must practice if you want to be good with impromptu speeches. You must put in the work and effort to reach a level of excellence. It is a very important skill, and it deserves every time and effort you put into it. If you practice, you will succeed.

CHAPTER ELEVEN

The Role of Memory

Memory... is the diary that we all carry about with us.
-Oscar Wilde

It shouldn't be a surprise that a chapter in this book is dedicated to the subject of memory. The most important aspect of any mental activity, such as the delivery of an impromptu speech, is the ability to recall and organize the needed information from your memory.

Have you ever been in a situation where you were asked a question that you were very sure you've heard the answer before, but couldn't recall it? Or maybe you gave an answer, but your answer happened to be inaccurate, and you felt bad because you know you could do better. Our memory often disappoints us. If you are unable to recall an information that is urgently needed, especially during an impromptu speech, you will not give the best presentation. I don't think anybody would like to be in that position, especially during important moments. This could be avoided. You can choose to keep your memory in prime condition for top performance.

This is not a book on neuroscience or cognitive psychology, neither am I a neuroscientist. I believe that is a good thing because it removes the possibility of wandering into deep concepts on memory. This subject will be kept simple and as straightforward as possible; based on both my research and my personal experiences. This chapter centers on basic concepts of memory and highlights essential information relevant to keeping both the brain and mind in optimal condition for delivering impromptu speeches.

What Is Memory?

Memory is the human ability to recall what has been learned or experienced. Memory is the primary evidence that you have learned something in the past.

I remember one day, a very long time ago, when I met an old friend at a store. We were both excited to see each other, an excitement that was followed by a lengthy conversation. At the end of our meeting that day, we exchanged phone numbers. I wrote his phone number on a piece of paper. And then, on my way home, for some reason, I decided to memorize his number. I succeeded in memorizing the number, so I thought, and then discarded the paper, with the confidence that I have the number up there. Several days later, I needed to call my friend, and I was disappointed. I could not remember the same phone number I thought I memorized. I tried the best I could to recall the phone number, but it was a fruitless struggle.

I am sure you have been in a situation where you tried to recall an information but couldn't. It is always a painful experience. Now, imagine what life would be like if you are unable to recall the things that you've learned. It would be terrible.

It is often said that the average human does not use more than 10 percent of the brain capacity. Although many scientists have called this a myth and have argued otherwise. Some of them believe that we use almost 100 percent of our brain capacity. However, the message that the 10 percent myth tries to pass across is that most people underutilize the capacity of their brains. Most proponents of this myth try to encourage their audience to make the most of their brains.

It doesn't matter which theory you believe, what matters most is how you use your brain. Let's assume you believe the 10 percent theory. How effectively do you use the 10 percent? The goal is to make sure that whatever you have in the 10 percent of your brain that you've used up is there to stay and, most importantly, that it is accessible.

In my case, I am sure my friend's phone number was not

completely out of my brain, I just couldn't assess it.

Let us go a little bit further into the subject so that you can get a clearer understanding of the concept of memory. I will start by highlighting the different kinds of memory and how they function.

Short-Term/Working Memory

Short-term memory is the human capacity for holding, but not manipulating, a small amount of information in mind in an active, readily available state for a short period. A research done by a cognitive psychologist George A. Miller in 1956 shows that the short-term memory can hold 7 +/- 2 items for less than a minute. He described this as The Magic Number 7 (Plus or Minus Two), which is often referred to as Miller's Law. This means that most adults can only hold about 5 to 9 items in their short-term memory at a time. For example, think of the words: Egg, Pawpaw, Vinegar, Cart, Crate, Boot, Cake, Almond, Ink, Kettle.

Looking at those words, you might not be able to recall the entire list at first glance. Even in most cases, at a second glance, it might still be difficult to remember all ten items. Let's say you can recall the list now; there is no guarantee that you will be able to list all ten items 24 hours from now. This is what George Miller tries to explain.

Although short-term memory cannot hold more than ten items for a long time, it serves a vital role as the gateway through which information gain access to long-term memory.

Also, short-term memory is said to be closely related to working memory. Unlike the short-term memory that only stores information, the working memory can manipulate information. The term "working memory" was also coined by George Miller and a team of other psychologists. According to Miller, the working memory has a limited capacity, and it plays an executive of processing and manipulation information. Working memory also plays an important role in reasoning.

Just imagine that you are in a panel where the subject of human trafficking is discussed. You start by making a case that poverty is the root cause of the problem. And then you begin to give points to support your claim, only to be interjected by a fellow discussant who believes that ignorance is the root cause. Then she starts to support her claim with what seems to be important points that sharply contradict your position. But deep down in your heart, you know that you are right about your claim and strongly believe you can prove it. While you listen to this rival, you are faced with two challenges: paying attention to what she is saying so that you can follow her argument and her position, and also holding on to your argument, the points you had in mind before you were interrupted and any additional point that could be useful in countering your opponent's points. At this point, your working memory is getting a workout! This is what the working memory is for; it helps you process and use information on the go.

The working memory plays an essential role in impromptu speaking and especially during a back and forth interactions like the example above.

Long-Term Memory

The long-term memory is used to store information over a long period of time. If you can remember something that happened or that you learned twenty-four hours ago, then it is in your long-term memory.

In theory, long-term memory has unlimited capacity, which means you can store as much information as you want to. Scientists have also argued that information stored in the long-term memory doesn't leave even though sometimes we can't remember them. That means when you hit a blank during an impromptu speech; it doesn't mean that the information has left your memory; it's just a case of poor impression or improper storage and, therefore, the difficulty in accessing it. Hence, the major constraint in recalling information from the long-term memory is not in its unavailability but rather its accessibility.

How Does Memory Work?

The human memory has a pattern of operation. It is important to understand this pattern of operation to improve its functionality. For example, when you meet somebody for the first time and the person tells you his or her name, and then you meet them a second time, the chances that you remember their name depends on how you stored the name in the first place.

There are three processes involved in memory; they are encoding, storage, and retrieval.

Encoding

To form new memories, information must be changed into a usable form, which occurs through the process known as encoding. An important part of encoding is attention. We cannot remember an event or activity that we did not pay attention to.

The way information is encoded plays a significant role on how quickly it is recalled. If you were very aware and alert when you had the experience, then the memory will probably be a lot more vivid.

Storage

What you want is a deep and lasting impression of any information you wish to retain. The information that we pay attention to and encode must be stored, first in the short-term memory, and then depending on the extent of exposure, it is moved to the long-term memory. Storage generally has to do with how the information is stored and how long it is stored. One crucial thing to remember is that the way we store information affects the way we retrieve it.

Take your computer as an example. If you store a file carelessly without proper consideration of what folder or what part of the computer it is stored, when the time comes for you to use that file, you might find it difficult to locate it. The difficulty in locating the file does not mean it is no longer on your computer; it is just a case of improper storage. For example, Abraham Lincoln read aloud to increase the impression of what he learned on his memory. When asked why he read aloud, he said: "When I read aloud, two senses catch the idea: first I see what I read; second, I hear it, and therefore I can remember it better." It is noted that his memory was extraordinarily retentive. This did not happen by chance; his style of learning made it possible.

Retrieval
Information stored in your memory would be useless to us if you do not retrieve it in your lifetime. But the truth is that at one point or another, you attempt to retrieve stored items for use. When you speak, there is a constant retrieval of information from your memory as you state your points, make your case, or share your message. When retrieval is difficult, you struggle to speak fluently.

Memories that you access very often are much easier to recall. On the other hand, memories that you don't recall often can be weakened or, in worse cases, lost as some other scientists argue. But don't forget that the manner and the strength of the impression of information on the memory determine how easy it would be to retrieve.

Improving Memory Performance
To be effective at impromptu speaking, you must go through mental workouts to keep all the forms of memory active and ready for action at all times. You must make an effort to maximize retention and minimize the loss of important information. To get better at this, you must strive to continuously improve the performance of your memory. In this regard, I will address some memorization techniques, because they help to improve retention ability and increase the performance of the memory.

Memorization Techniques
The use of memorization techniques in learning is also referred to as mnemonics. The use of these techniques increases

retention and the ease of retrieving information from memory. We can define memorization as the process of committing information to memory or the mental process of storing information in our memory to be recalled later.

Because of the relevance of memorization in learning, several principles and techniques have been developed and used over the years to aid this process of memorization.

Chunking

Let's go back to the items I listed earlier. Egg, Pawpaw, Vinegar, Cart, Crate, Boot, Cake, Almond, Ink, Kettle. Let us assume you are told to get these items from the store, and you are not allowed to write them down, how will you do it? I don't know about you, but it will be difficult for me to hold all ten items in my memory. However, with chunking, I can do it. With chunking, you can form acronyms with the first letter of each item. In this case, I made up VIP BAKE 3C. This is a better way to remember all ten items.

With the above example, we can define chunking as the process of breaking long pieces of information into groups or chunks. By doing this, you can increase the amount of information that you can store and ultimately remember. We use this method often. For example, when you want to commit the numbers 4162031923 to memory, you could rearrange it as 416 203 1923. So instead of trying to remember ten random digits, you have just three smaller groups of numbers that are easier to remember.

Chunking is used a lot in schools. For example, ROYGBIV is used to represent the colors that are separated when light is passed through a spectrum i.e., red, orange, yellow, green, blue, indigo, and violet. Also, BODMAS is used to represent the steps for solving a mathematical equation, and it stands for bracket, off, division, multiplication, addition, subtraction.

Rote Learning

This is a method that focuses not on understanding but merely on memorization through repetition. Rote learning is used mostly to aid the mastery of foundational knowledge. For example, the multiplication table in mathematics is mostly memorized through rote learning.

Rhyming System

This is another way to memorize information, especially a list. I once listened to a child recite the 66 books of the Holy Bible in the correct order by framing them into a rhyme. Ordinarily, that would have been an arduous task to assign to the memory. Also, as a teenager, I learned the first twenty elements of the periodic table with the help of a rhyme.

The Chain Method

This method is also known as The Link Method. It involves creating an association between items in a list. For example, on a basic level, to memorize the list: dog, car, bread, wristwatch and traffic, you could say; I took my dog with me in my car to a store to get bread. Looking at my wristwatch I was running late, so I increased my speed to avoid traffic during rush hours. It is argued that the story would be easier to remember than the list itself.

A simpler form of this method would be associating the information that you intend to commit to memory with one that has already been committed to memory. As such, when you try to retrieve one, you also retrieve the other. For example, for some reason, I had a problem recalling the last name of the founder of Kentucky Fried Chicken, Colonel Harland David Sanders. Popularly known as Colonel Sanders. I always remembered his title "Colonel" but always struggled with the last name, "Sanders." What I simply did was link the name Sanders with sandals. That was the last day I struggled to remember that name.

There are several other memorization techniques that can be used to enhance memorization. But the central idea behind using these mnemonics is to encode complex or difficult information in a manner that makes it easy to remember.

The Role of Memory

Please remember that the reason why I shared these techniques with you is because it is important to retain and easily recall the things that you learn, which is essential to be effective when speaking impromptu.

Keeping the Brain Active and Healthy

The brain is that important organ in your body that houses the memory. The healthiness of the brain determines how effective your memory would be. Knowing this, you should pay careful attention to the way you treat your brain. Always ensure to subject your brain to activities that will enhance its performance. I will discuss some habits that can greatly enhance the performance of your brain. Below are some useful suggestions.

Physical Exercise

Treating your body well, with enough exercise will do a lot of good to your brain. Engaging regularly in aerobic exercises will improve your memory and enhance your ability to process and recall information.

Physical exercises increase the flow of blood to the brain, which also increases the transportation of oxygen and other relevant nutrients to the brain cells. This also helps to reduce the risk of brain disorders and memory loss.

Your brain needs oxygen and other nutrients to function maximally. When the oxygen level in your brain is low, it affects your ability to concentrate, which in turn makes it more difficult to learn new information or recall information that you've learned.

Healthy diet

The functionality of your brain can be affected by what and how you eat. When you cut down on healthy foods, your body starts to conserve energy. When energy conservation is taking place, energy for complex thought is diminished.

The food you eat helps to fuel your brain for proper performance. When it comes down to diet and brain performance, you must not only look out for foods that are healthy for the brain, you must also look out for foods that negatively affect brain performance.

Just as there are foods that are good for the brain, there are also foods that tend to slow down the performance of the brain. Prominent among them are those foods containing saturated fats. Animal products are sources of saturated fat; like, red meat, whole milk, butter, cheese, etc. It was discovered in a research that rats that were fed with a high level of saturated fat did very poorly in learning and memory tests.

Certain foods are particularly helpful in improving your brain function. Many of these foods protect your brain by releasing antioxidants. The antioxidants that are released by these foods help to breakdown harmful substances (oxidants) naturally produced by the body. Most of these foods also contain important vitamins and nutrients essential for a sharp and healthy brain.

The following are brain foods that will help improve your memory:

Healthy Fats/ Omega-3 (cold-water fish, flax seed oil, soybeans, walnuts, and eggs etc. are all sources of Omega-3 fatty acid. Antioxidants, High-Tyrosine Proteins (seafood, meat, eggs, soy and dairy), Water, and Fibre (dried fruits, vegetables, legumes, nuts and seeds, whole fruit, whole grains).

Sleep and Memory

Several scientific researches show a positive relationship between memory performance and sleep. Sleep has also been known to have a profound impact on learning. A sleep-deprived person cannot focus their attention optimally and, therefore, cannot learn efficiently. Sleep also has a role in the consolidation of memory, which is essential for learning new information.

Brain Exercises

Here, I refer to brain activities as every possible exercise that engages and tasks the brain, especially taking it through unfamiliar activities and subjects. This could include learning to play a musical instrument, learning a new language, solving puzzles, playing board games, taking up video gaming, etc.

Feed Your Brain
Your brain is much like a computer (only better). And as you know, a computer can only give out information that has been feed into it. Consequently, your brain can deliver to you what you have properly stored in it. While you keep your brain healthy and active and while you have several memorization strategies at your disposal, it is important to take advantage of this and feed your brain with useful information, both those that are relevant in your area of specialization and those that keep you current as it relates to your immediate environment and the world.

The more subjects with which you're familiar, the easier it will be for you to deliver an impromptu speech. The truth is that if you're not interested in the world, the world is not going to be interested in you.

No matter the situation, whether you are having a conversation in a networking event or you are dealing with people in your job, the more you know about what is going on in the world, the more effective and interesting you will be. This doesn't mean that you should try to be an expert on all subjects. At least have enough knowledge about a variety of topics that you can have meaningful conversations about them.

The more you feed your brain, the more material you have for your impromptu speeches. Below are some suggestions on how to feed your mind and build your knowledge base.
1. Read books. One suggestion is to set a goal on the number of books to read, maybe in a week a month or a year. You could also listen to audiobooks or other educational material during your commute. This is a good use of your commute time. It will improve your knowledge about your career, your knowledge about what is going on in the world, and your ability to communicate effectively.

2. Stay up to date with the news. Go through the headlines and read stories that are most interesting or important to you.

3. Get involved in productive conversations. Broaden the scope of your conversations to other subject matter. If all you used to talks about was sports, you could start having conversations about politics, entertainment, lifestyle, etc. This will help build a broader knowledge base.

4. Live a versatile life. The more life experiences you have, the more interesting stories you can share with your audience. So, go to places you've not been before; different states, or country or vacation destinations. Have you played golf before? If not, try it out. Learn about a new sport. Go fishing, if you've never fished before. The list is endless. And don't forget to engage in meaningful conversations with people of different backgrounds, experiences, and ideologies, as you explore life.

Don't Neglect Your Memory

When you open your mouth to speak, everything you say comes from your memory. The vocabulary you use, your suggestions in discussions, your ideas all stem from your memory. If you think about this, you will understand while your memory is an asset in any intellectual endeavor and why I had to treat the subject of memory in a book on impromptu speaking. Always seek to enhance the performance of your memory, keep your brain active and healthy, and feed it with as much information as possible. Once again, remember that your ability to recall learned information quickly is essential for effective impromptu speaking. When you make an effort to improve the performance of your memory, you will excel when you are asked to speak without notice.

CHAPTER TWELVE

Tying the Knots Together

We are each other's harvest; we are each other's business; we are each other's magnitude and bond
-Gwendolyn Brooks

We have come a long way together. And in our journey together, I have tried to open your eyes to different concepts, ideas, and tricks that are relevant to set you on a spring board for a leap into the realm of excellence and away from the crowd, away from mediocrity in the art of speaking. Not just any form of speaking but speaking in moments when you are not prepared.

The ideas that you've gleaned in this book should not stand in isolation. Just as one tree cannot make a forest, two people cannot work together except they agree. The renowned author J.K Rowling said it correctly, "We are only strong as we are united, as weak as we are divided." This means that these concepts and ideas must stick and work together for you to achieve your goals as a brilliant speaker. What is the use to have a roadmap for a journey that you lack the confidence to embark on? Or what would you do with brick and mortar if you don't have plans to erect a structure? These concepts must, therefore, come together to make complete sense.

Although our concepts are dispersed across several chapters, I attempt in this chapter to bring all the pieces together to help you make sense of it all. Seeing the subject lined up just behind each other in what would be a summary, will go a long way to remind you of what you have learned and reinforce your understanding of the subject.

Take note of the following:

You Are Not Alone

Are you angry with yourself because you are not outstanding when called to speak without notice? I think it is ok to be angry with yourself, but this anger should be for the right reasons, maybe because you crave the need for excellence in public speaking or perhaps some other important reasons. But it should never be because you feel you are the only one with this problem. That would be ridiculous. Just take comfort from the fact that you are not alone. There is a vast global community of people who also struggle to put their thought together when they are placed on the spot. Be happy because there is room for improvement.

Fight Your Greatest Enemy

Generally, as far as speaking in public is concerned, your greatest enemy is not your audience, as you may be tempted to think. In fact, many people believe that your audience could even be praying for you to succeed. Your greatest enemy is fear!!! Your greatest enemy is just that abstract concept of fear. It is so amazing how fear sneaks into our beautiful minds and makes a mess of our entire body mechanism. You mustn't allow fear to get into you when you are called upon to speak, for fear is just a mirage. You can manage it effectively and watch yourself soar as an outstanding speaker.

Remember the Pattern

Speeches are not just delivered anyhow we want it, and in any order we please. The togetherness and coherence you hear when you listen to a good impromptu speech are born out of a well-structured speech pattern. There is an order to every good speech. This order takes the form of an introduction, a body, and a conclusion. It is in the body of the speech that you state your points and the points must be consolidated with supporting examples. When you frame your impromptu speech in this order, it makes it sensible and logical.

Don't Move Without a Plan
The importance of planning cannot be overstressed. As it is important in any of life's endeavor, so also it is important in impromptu speeches. Some several plans or strategies can be used to make your impromptu speech easy to deliver. You could use the "past, present, future," "cause, effect, remedy," "PREP Method," or "before, the event, the result" strategy. There are other strategies not mentioned here. They are all essential. They form effective frameworks upon which you lay the content of your speech.

Use Strong Building Blocks
What can you say without language? Language is the basic unit of communication. This is what shapes our understanding of the world and everything that exists around us. For a good impromptu speech, your language must be effective and in the right order and manner for the benefit of your audience and for a more impactful message. According to Dale Carnegie, your purpose is to make your audience see what you saw, hear what you heard, feel what you felt. It is only a good use of language that can make this possible. You must also remember that a language that is right for one audience can be wrong for another audience. This is important to note because the audience is the most important element of the mix.

Don't Go Naked
Also, a significant part of language is style. Stylistic devices, as they are sometimes referred to, are available to adorn a speech. Think of style as the effect fashion has on a person's outlook. When they are slack or when they don't fit, it makes the wearer look dull and unattractive. But on the other hand, when they are a perfect fit and nicely tailored, they make the wearer look smart and attractive. This is what style does to a speech. Also, styles can make your speech very memorable, causing it to stick with the audience by creating patterns in their minds.

Open Your Ears

Open your ears, listen, and you will learn. You will learn even from those who talk badly, Plutarch tells us. Listening is also crucial in the subject of impromptu speaking, for with it, you enhance and broaden your knowledge. This also includes knowledge gained during the event or within the space where you are called upon to speak. Your response to an issue can be flawed within a gathering just because you have not been following along or listening to the things that are been said. So, it is very important to listen; it puts you at an advantage.

Strike With Vengeance

According to the English novelist David Herbert Lawrence, "Be still when you have nothing to say; when genuine passion moves you, say what you've got to say, and say it hot." This is what a good delivery is about. When you give an impromptu speech, ensure that you put out a powerful delivery that would convey your words in the most effective and impactful way. Think of your eye contact, your gesture, your voice, your speaking rate. And don't forget to pause to let your message sink in.

Become a Judge

As far as speaking is concerned, being a critic is a good thing. The more you evaluate and critic other speeches, the more knowledge you have about what works and what doesn't work in an impromptu speech, and the better you get at speaking off the cuff. But remember, your duty is not just to evaluate the speeches of other people; you must also evaluate your own speech; from audio and video recordings of yourself. When critiquing, you must ensure to evaluate every aspect of the speech, the content, the structure, and the delivery components.

If you are in a position to give feedback to a speaker, make sure you do this effectively, in such a manner that the lessons learned are actionable.

Tying the Knots Together

This Is Not Magic

Excellence does not come cheap; you must embrace this truth. To attain excellence in delivering impromptu speeches, you must practice. Practice! Practice!! Practice!!! When you commit yourself to practice, excellence will give itself to you. As we mentioned, your practice should not be mindless. You must engage in deliberate practice to get maximum results and benefits. You could have a list of different kinds of impromptu topics and randomly pick and discuss them. You can also randomly discuss issues on news or television as the case maybe. You could also join a Toastmasters club.

Maintain Your Storehouse

Your memory is your storehouse. It must be kept in order. What is the use of language? Why would you think of a strategy for your speech? Confidence won't even be of much use if you have absolutely nothing to say. It is from your memory that you draw out the content for your speech. And the healthier and more vibrant your mind and memory, the richer the quality of the content of your speech, and the more informative it would be. Therefore, you must pay special attention to your memory, how it functions, and how you can improve its performance. And do not forget to feed it.

Sticks in a Bundle Are Unbreakable

"Sticks in a bundle are unbreakable" is a Kenyan proverb. This statement is true. As I have stated at the beginning of this chapter, the ideas that you have learned cannot be left in isolation if you must reach a level of excellence in the art of impromptu speaking. There is a need to understand and master every concept that has been addressed in other to get the desired result.

It has been a pleasurable ride for me, and I guess you feel the same way too. I believe that a lot has been learned, but what you must understand is that beyond this knowledge is the need for you to act, the need for you to go out and explore, the need to conquer. My desire is that you are outstanding every single time you are called upon to speak without notice.

To your success!!!

PRACTICE TOPICS

Work It Out

Good things come to those who sweat.
-Anonymous

30 One Word Topics

Family -Love -Friends -Music -Work -Careers -Christmas -
Marriage -Movies -Crime -Clothes -Fashion -Internet -
Courage -Religion -Dating -Money -Shopping -Abortion -War
-Games -Smoking -School -Art -Relationships -Forgiveness -
Kindness -Leadership -Victory -Pride

Quotations

1. "They always say time changes things, but you actually have to change them yourself." – Andy Warhol
2. "We did not change as we grew older; we just became more clearly ourselves." – Lynn Hall
3. "The more things change, the more they remain… insane." – Michael Fry and T. Lewis
4. "The whole of science is nothing more than a refinement of everyday thinking." – Einstein
5. "I respect faith, but doubt is what gets you an education." – Wilson Mizner
6. "The best way to predict the future is to invent it." – Alan Kay
7. "To live a creative life, we must lose our fear of being wrong." – Joseph Chilton Pearce
8. "Excellence is the best deterrent to racism or sexism." – Oprah Winfrey
9. "There can be as much value in the blink of an eye as in months of rational analysis." – Malcom Gladwell
10. "The dead cannot cry out for justice; it is a duty of the

living to do so for them." – Lois McMaster Bujold

11. "Woman is woman's natural ally." – Euripides
12. "It is not true that equality is a law of nature. Nature has no equality. Its sovereign law is subordination and dependence." – Marquis de Vauvenargues
13. "Let thy speech be better than silence or be silent." - Dionysius Of Halicarnassus
14. "Technological progress has merely provided us with more efficient means of going backwards." – Aldous Huxley
15. "In order that all men may be taught to speak truth, it is necessary that all likewise should learn to hear it." – Samuel Johnson
16. "We are inclined to believe those whom we do not know because they have never deceived us." – Samuel Johnson
17. "Morality, like art, means drawing a line someplace." – Oscar Wilde
18. "A little sincerity is a dangerous thing, and a great deal of it is absolutely fatal." – Oscar Wilde
19. "Advertising is the modern substitute for argument; its function is to make the worse appear the better." – George Santayana
20. "The truth will set you free. But first, it will piss you off." – Gloria Steinem
21. "There are three kinds of lies: lies, damned lies, and statistics." – Benjamin Disareli

Other Topics

22. What is the biggest effect of the internet?
23. Can technology answer the problems of modern society?
24. How is human overpopulation affecting modern-day society?
25. Describe your worst experience.
26. Describe the most memorable event in your life.
27. What is the current most difficult global challenge?

28. Discuss your opinion about marriage.
29. What are the qualities of a good leader?
30. What invention has had the greatest impact on your life?
31. How does availability or lack of money affect a person's personality?
32. What can be done to stop the violence in this country?
33. What would the world be like 50 years from now?
34. Would you rather be a political leader or a business leader?
35. Why is it important to constantly upgrade the standard of education in the world?
36. What do you think can be done to stop human trafficking?
37. Where do you find inspiration?
38. Can you describe your life in a six-word sentence?
39. If we learn from our mistakes, why are we always so afraid to make a mistake?
40. What impact do you want to leave on the world?
41. What is the most defining moment of your life thus far?
42. In the haste of your daily life, what are you not seeing?
43. If life is so short, why do we do so many things we don't like and like so many things we don't do?
44. What lifts your spirits when life gets you down?
45. Have you ever regretted something you did not say or do?
46. Has your greatest fear ever come true?
47. Why do we think of others the most when they're gone?
48. What is your most beloved childhood memory?
49. Is it more important to love or be loved?
50. If it all came back around to you, would it help you or hurt you?
51. If you had the chance to go back in time and change one thing would you do it?
52. If a doctor gave you five years to live, what would you

try to accomplish?

53. What is the difference between falling in love and being in love?
54. Who do you think stands between you and happiness?
55. What is the difference between innocence and ignorance?
56. What is the simplest truth you can express in words?
57. What gives your life meaning?
58. Can there be happiness without sadness? Pleasure without pain? Peace without war?
59. What's the one thing you'd like others to remember about you at the end of your life?
60. Is there such a thing as perfect?
61. To what degree have you actually controlled the course your life has taken?
62. What does it mean to be human?
63. If you looked into the heart of your enemy, what do you think you would find that is different from what is in your own heart?
64. What do you love most about yourself?
65. Where would you most like to go and why?
66. Is it more important to do what you love or to love what you are doing?
67. What do you imagine yourself doing ten years from now?
68. What small act of kindness were you once shown that you will never forget?
69. What is your happiest childhood memory? What makes it so special?
70. Do you own your things or do your things own you?
71. Would you rather lose all of your old memories or never be able to make new ones?
72. How do you deal with someone in a position of power who wants you to fail?
73. What do you have that you cannot live without?
74. When you close your eyes what do you see?
75. What sustains you on a daily basis?

76. What are your top five personal values?
77. Why must you love someone enough to let them go?
78. Do you ever celebrate the green lights?
79. What personal prisons have you built out of fears?
80. What one thing have you not done that you really want to do?
81. Why are you, you?
82. If you haven't achieved it yet what do you have to lose?
83. What three words would you use to describe the last three months of your life?
84. Is it ever right to do the wrong thing? Is it ever wrong to do the right thing?
85. How would you describe 'freedom' in your own words?
86. What is the most important thing you could do right now in your personal life?
87. If you could ask one person, alive or dead, only one question, who would you ask and what would you ask?
88. If happiness was the national currency, what kind of work would make you rich?
89. What is your number one goal for the next six months?
90. Would you ever give up your life to save someone else?
91. Are you happy with yourself?
92. What is the meaning of 'peace' to you?
93. What are three moral rules you will never break?
94. What does it mean to allow another person to truly love you?
95. Who or what do you think of when you think of love?
96. If your life was a novel, what would be the title and how would your story end?
97. What would you not give up for $1,000,000 in cash?
98. When do you feel most like yourself?
99. When you help someone do you ever think, "What's in it for me?"
100. What is your greatest challenge?
https://dist8tm.org

Personal Story Mining

The first stage of personal story mining is to recall personal life stories that speak to issues/topics in the world. Remember, these could be stories of your own life experiences, stories of events you witnessed, stories about the experience of people you know, etc.

Make sure to write out the stories. Don't assume you have them in your memory. Do the work and fill out these blank pages with your stories. You can use extra notes if you have multiple stories for one item.

Dig into your memory and start mining. ↓

Hard work

_____

_____

_____

_____

_____

_____

_____

_____

_____

_____

_____

_____

_____

Work it out

Resilience

_____

_____

_____

_____

_____

_____

_____

_____

_____

_____

_____

_____

_____

_____

_____

_____

_____

_____

_____

_____

_____

_____

_____

_____

Courage

_____

_____

_____

_____

_____

_____

_____

_____

_____

_____

_____

_____

_____

_____

_____

_____

_____

_____

_____

_____

_____

_____

_____

_____

Work it out

Patience

Kindness

Work it out

Empathy

_____

_____

_____

_____

_____

_____

_____

_____

_____

_____

_____

_____

_____

_____

_____

_____

_____

_____

_____

_____

_____

Anger

_____

_____

_____

_____

_____

_____

_____

_____

_____

_____

_____

_____

_____

_____

_____

_____

_____

_____

_____

_____

_____

_____

_____

Work it out

Jealousy

_____

_____

_____

_____

_____

_____

_____

_____

_____

_____

_____

_____

_____

_____

_____

_____

_____

_____

_____

Greed

_____

_____

_____

_____

_____

_____

_____

_____

_____

_____

_____

_____

_____

_____

_____

_____

_____

_____

_____

_____

_____

_____

_____

_____

_____

_____

Work it out

Hatred

_____

_____

_____

_____

_____

_____

_____

_____

_____

_____

_____

_____

_____

_____

_____

_____

_____

_____

_____

_____

_____

_____

_____

_____

Friendship

Forgiveness

_____

_____

_____

_____

_____

_____

_____

_____

_____

_____

_____

_____

_____

_____

_____

_____

_____

_____

_____

_____

_____

_____

Gratitude

Work it out

Loyalty

_____

_____

_____

_____

_____

_____

_____

_____

_____

_____

_____

_____

_____

_____

_____

_____

_____

_____

_____

_____

_____

_____

_____

_____

Funny story about your name

_____

_____

_____

_____

_____

_____

_____

_____

_____

_____

_____

_____

_____

_____

_____

_____

_____

_____

_____

_____

_____

_____

Work it out

Funny story of a wardrobe malfunction

Funny story about your accent

_____

_____

_____

_____

_____

_____

_____

_____

_____

_____

_____

_____

_____

_____

_____

_____

_____

_____

_____

_____

_____

Work it out

Funny story about _____

_____

_____

_____

_____

_____

_____

_____

_____

_____

_____

_____

_____

_____

_____

_____

_____

_____

_____

_____

_____

_____

Intelligence

_____

_____

_____

_____

_____

_____

_____

_____

_____

_____

_____

_____

_____

_____

_____

_____

_____

_____

_____

_____

_____

_____

_____

Work it out

Ambition

_____

_____

_____

_____

_____

_____

_____

_____

_____

_____

_____

_____

_____

_____

_____

_____

_____

_____

_____

_____

Wealth

_____

_____

_____

_____

_____

_____

_____

_____

_____

_____

_____

_____

_____

_____

_____

_____

_____

_____

_____

_____

_____

_____

Work it out

Poverty

_____

_____

_____

_____

_____

_____

_____

_____

_____

_____

_____

_____

_____

_____

_____

_____

_____

_____

_____

_____

_____

_____

Guilt

Work it out

A bad weather experience

_____

_____

_____

_____

_____

_____

_____

_____

_____

_____

_____

_____

_____

_____

_____

_____

_____

_____

_____

_____

_____

_____

Story about_____

_____

_____

_____

_____

_____

_____

_____

_____

_____

_____

_____

_____

_____

_____

_____

_____

_____

_____

_____

_____

_____

_____

_____

Work it out

Story about_____

_____

_____

_____

_____

_____

_____

_____

_____

_____

_____

_____

_____

_____

_____

_____

_____

_____

_____

_____

_____

_____

_____

_____

Story about_____

_____

_____

_____

_____

_____

_____

_____

_____

_____

_____

_____

_____

_____

_____

_____

_____

_____

_____

_____

_____

_____

_____

_____

_____

_____

Work it out

Story about_____

_____
_____
_____
_____
_____
_____
_____
_____
_____
_____
_____
_____
_____
_____
_____
_____
_____
_____
_____
_____
_____
_____
_____
_____

I hope you were able to write as many stories as you can. For some people, this assignment is easy to do; for some other people, it could be a challenge. Going back to your past to recall stories can be difficult, but it is worth the effort.

Now that you have these stories, you need to structure them so that they are compelling when told during conversations, impromptu speeches, and prepared speeches.

ABOUT THE AUTHOR

Solomon Asine is the founder and lead instructor at Home of Influence, a company that helps individuals and businesses reach a high level of competence in persuasive communication and social intelligence.
For almost a decade, Solomon has trained thousands of people on subjects like public speaking, social intelligence, vocal quality improvement, impromptu speaking, and other related topics.

For questions, comments, or coaching, contact the author at solomon@homeofinfluence.com

Your Voice Matters!

I hope you've found "Think Fast Speak Smart" to be a worthy companion on your journey to becoming an exceptional impromptu speaker. Your feedback is incredibly important, as it helps me continue to improve and inspire others. If you've gained valuable insights on impromptu speaking through this book, I would love to hear from you.

Scan the quick response (QR) code below to share your thoughts

Your review not only helps me understand your needs better but also enables me to reach and empower more individuals seeking to enhance their impromptu speaking abilities.

Thank you for being a part of the community and for choosing "Think Fast Speak Smart" as your guide. Your words have the power to inspire others to embark on their own journey to brilliance.

Remember, your voice matters, and your feedback is greatly appreciated. Keep speaking smart and shining bright!

With heartfelt appreciation,

Solomon Asine

90550539R00100